Fashions in Literature

FASHIONS IN LITERATURE

And Other Literary and Social Essays & Addresses

By CHARLES DUDLEY WARNER

INTRODUCTION BY
Hamilton Wright Mabie

Essay Index Reprint Series

 BOOKS FOR LIBRARIES PRESS
FREEPORT, NEW YORK

First Published 1902
Reprinted 1970

INTERNATIONAL STANDARD BOOK NUMBER:
0-8369-1857-6

LIBRARY OF CONGRESS CATALOG CARD NUMBER:
72-128328

PRINTED IN THE UNITED STATES OF AMERICA

Table of Contents

[v]

TABLE OF CONTENTS

Introduction

THIRTY years ago and more those who read and valued good books in this country made the acquaintance of Mr. Warner, and since the publication of "My Summer In a Garden" no work of his has needed any other introduction than the presence of his name on the titlepage; and now that reputation has mellowed into memory, even the word of interpretation seems superfluous.   Mr. Warner wrote out of a clear, as well as a full mind, and lucidity of style was part of that harmonious charm of sincerity and urbanity which made him one of the most intelligible and companionable of our writers.

It is a pleasure, however, to recall him as, not long ago, we saw him move and heard him speak in the ripeness of years which brought him the full flavour of maturity without any loss of freshness from his humour or serenity from his thought.   He shared

with Lowell, Longfellow, and Curtis a har-
mony of nature and art, a unity of ideal and
achievement, which make him a welcome
figure, not only for what he said, but for what
he was; one of those friends whose coming
is hailed with joy because they seem always
at their best, and minister to rather than
draw upon our own capital of moral vitality.

Mr. Warner was the most undogmatic
of idealists, the most winning of teachers.
He had always something to say to the ethical sense, a word for the conscience; but his
approach was always through the mind, and
his enforcement of the moral lesson was by
suggestion rather than by commandment.
There was nothing ascetic about him, no
easy solution of the difficulties of life by ignoring or evading them; nor, on the other
hand, was there any confusion of moral
standards as the result of a confusion of
ideas touching the nature and functions of
art. He saw clearly, he felt deeply, and he
thought straight; hence the rectitude of his
mind, the sanity of his spirit, the justice of
his dealings with the things which make for

life and art. He used the essay as Addison used it, not for sermonic effect, but as a form of art which permitted a man to deal with serious things in a spirit of gayety, and with that lightness of touch which conveys influence without employing force. He was as deeply enamoured as George William Curtis with the highest ideals of life for America, and, like Curtis, his expression caught the grace and distinction of those ideals.

It is a pleasure to hear his voice once more, because its very accents suggest the most interesting, high-minded, and captivating ideals of living; he brings with him that air of fine breeding which is diffused by the men who, in mind as in manners, have been, in a distinctive sense, gentlemen; who have lived so constantly and habitually on intimate terms with the highest things in thought and character that the tone of this really best society has become theirs. Among men of talent there are plebeians as well as patricians; even genius, which is never vulgar, is sometimes unable to hide the vulgarity of the aims and ideas which it clothes with beauty without concealing their essential nature. Mr. Warner was a patrician; the most democratic of men, he was one of the most fastidious in his intellectual companionships and affiliations.

The subjects about which he speaks with his old-time directness and charm in this volume make us aware of the serious temper of his mind, of his deep interest in the life of his time and people, and of the easy and natural grace with which he insisted on facing the fact and bringing it to the test of the highest standards. In his discussion of "Fashions in Literature" he deftly brings before us the significance of literature and the signs which it always wears, while he seems bent upon considering some interesting aspects of contemporary writing.

And how admirably he has described his own work in his definition of qualities which are common to all literature of a high order: simplicity, knowledge of human nature, agreeable personality. It would be impossible in briefer or more comprehensive phrase to sum up and express the secret of his influence and of the pleasure he gives us. It is to suggest this application of his words to himself that this preparatory comment is written.

When "My Summer In a Garden" appeared, it won a host of friends who did not stop to ask whether it was a piece of excellent journalism or a bit of real literature. It was so natural, so informal, so intimate that readers accepted it as matter of course, as they accepted the blooming of flowers and the flitting of birds. It was simply a report of certain things which had happened out of doors, made by an observing neighbour whose talk seemed to be of a piece with the diffused fragrance and light and life of the old-fashioned garden. This easy approach, along natural lines of interest, by quietly putting himself on common ground with his reader, Mr. Warner never abandoned; he was so delightful a companion that until he ceased to walk beside them, many of his friends of the mind did not realise how much he had enriched them by the way. This charming simplicity, which made it possible for him to put himself on intimate terms with his readers, was the result of his sincerity, his clearness of thought, and his ripe culture: that knowledge of the best which rids a man forever of faith in devices, dexterities, obscurities, and all other substitutes for the lucid realities of thinking and of character.

To his love of reality and his sincere interest in men, Mr. Warner added natural shrewdness and long observation of the psychology of men and women under the stress and strain of experience. His knowledge of human nature did not lessen his geniality, but it kept the edge of his mind keen, and gave his work the variety not only of humour but of satire. He cared deeply for people, but they did not impose on him; he loved his country with a passion which was the more genuine because it was exacting and, at times, sharply critical. There runs through all his work, as a critic of manners and men, as well as of art, a wisdom of life born of wide and keen observation; put not into the form of aphorisms, but of shrewd comment, of keen criticism, of nice discrimination between the manifold shadings of insincerity, of insight into the action and reaction of conditions, surroundings, social and ethical aims on men and women. The stories written in his later years are full of the evidences of a knowledge of human nature which was singularly trustworthy and penetrating.

When all has been said, however, it remains true of him, as of so many of the writers whom we read and love and love as we read, that the secret of his charm lay in an agreeable personality. At the end of the analysis, if the work is worth while, there is always a man, and the man is the explanation of the work. This is preeminently true of those writers whose charm lies less in distinctively intellectual qualities than in temperament, atmosphere, humour, — writers of the quality of Steele, Goldsmith, Lamb, Irving. It is not only, therefore, a pleasure to recall Mr. Warner; it is a necessity if one would discover the secret of his charm, the source of his authority.

He was a New Englander by birth and by long residence, but he was also a man of the world in the true sense of the phrase;

one whose ethical judgment had been broadened without being lowered; who had learned that truth, though often strenuously enforced, is never so convincing as when stated in terms of beauty; and to whom it had been revealed that to live naturally, sanely, and productively one must live humanly, with due regard to the earthly as well as to heavenly, with ease as well as earnestness of spirit, through play no less than through work, in the large resources of art, society, and humour, as well as with the ancient and well-tested rectitudes of the fathers.

The harmonious play of his whole nature, the breadth of his interests and the sanity of his spirit made Mr. Warner a delightful companion, and kept to the very end the freshness of his mind and the spontaneity of his humour; life never lost its savour for him, nor did his style part with its diffused but thoroughly individual humour. This latest collection of his papers, dealing with a wide range of subjects from the " Education of the Negro" to " Literature and the Stage," with characteristic comments on " Truthfulness" and "The Pursuit of Happiness," shows him at the end of his long and tireless career as a writer still deeply interested in contemporary events, responsive to the appeal of the questions of the hour, and sensitive to all things which affected the dignity and authority of literature. In his interests, his bearing, his relations to the public life of the country, no less than in his work, he held fast to the best traditions of literature, and he has taken his place among the representative American men of Letters.

HAMILTON W. MABIE.

Fashions in Literature

IF you examine a collection of prints of costumes of different generations, you are commonly amused by the ludicrous appearance of most of them, especially of those that are not familiar to you in your own decade. They are not only inappropriate and inconvenient to your eye, but they offend your taste. You cannot believe that they were ever thought beautiful and becoming. If your memory does not fail you, however, and you retain a little honesty of mind, you can recall the fact that a costume which seems to you ridiculous to-day had your warm approval ten years ago. You wonder, indeed, how you could ever have tolerated a costume which has not one graceful line, and has no more relation to the human figure than Mambrino's helmet had

I

to a crown of glory. You cannot imagine how you ever approved the vast balloon skirt that gave your sweetheart the appearance of the great bell of Moscow, or that you yourself could have been complacent in a coat the tails of which reached your heels, and the buttons of which, a rudimentary survival, were between your shoulder-blades — you who are now devoted to a female figure that resembles an old-fashioned churn surmounted by an isosceles triangle.

These vagaries of taste, which disfigure or destroy correct proportions or hide deformities, are nowhere more evident than in the illustrations of works of fiction. The artist who collaborates with the contemporary novelist has a hard fate. If he is faithful to the fashions of the day, he earns the repute of artistic depravity in the eyes of the next generation. The novel may become a classic, because it represents human nature, or even the whimsicalities of a period; but the illustrations of the artist only provoke a smile, because he has represented merely the unessential and the fleeting. The interest in his work is archæological, not artistic. The genius of the great portrait-painter may to some extent overcome the disadvantages of contemporary costume, but if the costume of his period is hideous and lacks the essential lines of beauty, his work is liable to need the apology of quaintness. The Greek artist and the mediæval painter, when the costumes were really picturesque and made us forget the lack of simplicity in a noble sumptuousness, had never this posthumous difficulty to contend with.

In the examination of costumes of different races and different ages, we are also struck by the fact that with primitive or isolated peoples costumes vary little from age to age, and fashion and the fashions are unrecognised, and a habit of dress which is dictated by climate, or has been proved to be comfortable, is adhered to from one generation to another; while nations that we call highly civilised, meaning commonly not only Occidental peoples, but peoples called progressive, are subject to the most frequent and violent changes of fashions, not in generations only, but in decades and years of a generation, as if the mass had no mind or taste of its own, but submitted to the irresponsible ukase of tailors and modistes, who are in alliance with enterprising manufacturers of novelties. In this higher civilisation a costume which is artistic and becoming has no more chance of permanence than one which is ugly and inconvenient. It might be inferred that this higher civilisation produces no better taste and discrimination, no more independent judgment, in dress than it does in literature. The vagaries in dress of the Western nations for a thousand years past, to go back no further, are certainly highly amusing, and would be humiliating to people who regarded taste and art as essentials of civilisation. But when we speak of civilisation, we cannot but notice that some of the great civilisations, the longest permanent and most notable for highest achievement in learning, science, art, or in the graces or comforts of life, the Egyptian, the Saracenic, the Chinese, were subject to no such vagaries in costume, but adhered to that which taste, climate, experience had determined to be the most useful and appropriate. And it is a singular comment upon our modern conceit that we make our own vagaries and changeableness, and not any fixed principles of art or of utility, the criterion of judgment on other races and other times.

The more important result of the study of past fashions, in engravings and paintings, remains to be spoken of. It is that in all the illustrations, from the simplicity of Athens, through the artificiality of Louis XIV and the monstrosities of Elizabeth, down to the undescribed modistic inventions of the first McKinley, there is discoverable a radical and primitive law of beauty. We acknowledge it among the Greeks, we encounter it in one age and another. I mean a style of dress that is artistic as well as picturesque, that satisfies our love of beauty, that accords with the grace of the perfect human figure, and that gives as perfect satisfaction to the cultivated taste as a drawing by Raphael. While all the other illustrations of the human ingenuity in making the human race appear fantastic or ridiculous amuse us or offend our taste, — except the tailor fashion-plates of the week that is now, — these few exceptions, classic or modern, give us permanent delight, and are recognised as following the eternal law of beauty and utility. And we know, notwithstanding the temporary triumph of bad taste and the public lack of any taste, that there is a standard, artistic and imperishable

The student of manners might find an interesting field in noting how, in our Occidental civilisations, fluctuations of opinions, of morals, and of literary style have been accompanied by more or less significant exhibitions of costumes. He will note in the *Précieux* of France and the Euphuist of England a corresponding effeminacy in dress; in the frank paganism of the French Revolution the affectation of Greek and Roman apparel, passing into the Directoire style in the Citizen and the Citizeness; in the Calvinistic cut of the Puritan of Geneva and of New England the grim severity of their theology and morals. These examples are interesting as showing an inclination to express an inner condition by the outward apparel, as the Quakers indicate an inward peace by an external drabness, and the American Indian a bellicose disposition by red and yellow paint; just as we express by red stripes our desire to kill men with artillery, or by yellow stripes to kill them with cavalry. It is not possible to say whether these external displays are relics of barbarism or are enduring necessities of human nature.

The fickleness of men in costume in a manner burlesques their shifty and uncertain taste in literature. A book or a certain fashion in letters will have a run like a garment, and, like that, will pass away before it waxes old. It seems incredible, as we look back over the literary history of the past three centuries only, what prevailing styles and moods of expression, affectations, and prettinesses, each in turn, have pleased reasonably cultivated people. What tedious and vapid things they read and liked to read! Think of the French, who had once had a Villon, intoxicating themselves with somnolent draughts of Richardson. But, then, the French could match the paste euphuisms of Lyly with the novels of Scudéry. Every modern literature has been subject to these epidemics and diseases. It is needless to dwell upon them in detail. Since the great diffusion of printing, these literary crazes have been more frequent and of shorter duration. We need go back no further than a generation to find abundant examples of eccentricities of style and expression, of crazes over some author or some book, as unaccountable on principles of art as many of the fashions in social life. The more violent the attack, the sooner it is over. Readers of middle age can recall the furor over Tupper, the extravagant expectations as to the brilliant essayist Gilfillan, the soon-extinguished hopes of the poet Alexander Smith. For the moment the world waited in the belief of the rising of new stars, and as suddenly realised that it had been deceived. Sometimes we like ruggedness, and again we like things made easy. Within

a few years a distinguished Scotch clergyman made a fortune by diluting a paragraph
written by Saint Paul. It is in our memory
how at one time all the boys tried to write
like Macaulay, and then like Carlyle, and
then like Ruskin, and we have lived to see
the day when all the girls would like to write
like Heine.

In less than twenty years we have seen
wonderful changes in public taste and in the
efforts of writers to meet it or to create it.
We saw the everlastingly revived conflict
between realism and romanticism. We saw
the realist run into the naturalist, the naturalist into the animalist, the psychologist
into the sexualist, and the sudden reaction
to romance, in the form of what is called
the historic novel, the receipt for which can
be prescribed by any competent pharmacist.
The one essential in the ingredients is that
the hero shall be only got out of one hole by
dropping him into a deeper one, until — the
proper serial length being attained — he is
miraculously dropped out into daylight, and
stands to receive the plaudits of a tender-

[9]

hearted world, that is fond of nothing so much as of fighting.

The extraordinary vogue of certain recent stories is not so much to be wondered at when we consider the millions that have been added to the readers of English during the past twenty-five years. The wonder is that a new book does not sell more largely, or it would be a wonder if the ability to buy kept pace with the ability to read, and if discrimination had accompanied the appetite for reading. The critics term these successes of some recent fictions "crazes," but they are really sustained by some desirable qualities — they are cleverly written, and they are for the moment undoubtedly entertaining. Some of them as undoubtedly appeal to innate vulgarity or to cultivated depravity. I will call no names, because that would be to indict the public taste. This recent phenomenon of sales of stories by the hundred thousand is not, however, wholly due to quality. Another element has come in since the publishers have awakened to the fact that literature can be treated like merchandise. To use their own phrase, they "handle" books as they would "handle" patent medicines, that is, the popular patent medicines that are desired because of the amount of alcohol they contain; indeed, they are sold along with dry-goods and fancy notions. I am not objecting to this great and wide distribution any more than I am to the haste of fruit-dealers to market their products before they decay. The wary critic will be very careful about dogmatising over the nature and distribution of literary products. It is no certain sign that a book is good because it is popular, nor is it any more certain that it is good because it has a very limited sale. Yet we cannot help seeing that many of the books that are the subject of crazes utterly disappear in a very short time, while many others, approved by only a judicious few, continue in the market and slowly become standards, considered as good stock by the booksellers and continually in a limited demand.

The English essayists have spent a good deal of time lately in discussing the question

whether it is possible to tell a good contemporary book from a bad one. Their
hesitation is justified by a study of English
criticism of new books in the quarterly,
monthly, and weekly periodicals from the
latter part of the eighteenth century to the
last quarter of the nineteenth; or, to name
a definite period, from the verse of the Lake
poets, from Shelley and Byron, down to
Tennyson, there is scarcely a poet who has
attained world-wide assent to his position in
the first or second rank who was not at the
hands of the reviewers the subject of mockery
and bitter detraction. To be original in any
degree was to be damned. And there is
scarcely one who was at first ranked as a
great light during this period who is now
known out of the biographical dictionary.
Nothing in modern literature is more amaz-
ing than the bulk of English criticism in the
last three quarters of a century, so far as it
concerned individual writers, both in poetry
and prose. The literary rancour shown rose
to the dignity almost of theological vitu-
peration.

Is there any way to tell a good book from a bad one? Yes. As certainly as you can tell a good picture from a bad one, or a good egg from a bad one. Because there are hosts who do not discriminate as to the eggs or the butter they eat, it does not follow that a normal taste should not know the difference. Because there is a highly artistic nation that welcomes the flavour of garlic in everything, and another which claims to be the most civilised in the world that cannot tell coffee from chicory, or because the ancient Chinese love rancid sesame oil, or the Esquimaux like spoiled blubber and tainted fish, it does not follow that there is not in the world a wholesome taste for things natural and pure.

It is clear that the critic of contemporary literature is quite as likely to be wrong as right. He is, for one thing, inevitably affected by the prevailing fashion of his little day. And, worse still, he is apt to make his own tastes and prejudices the standard of his judgment. His view is commonly provincial instead of cosmopolitan. In the English

period just referred to it is easy to see that
most of the critical opinion was determined
by political or theological animosity and
prejudice. The rule was for a Tory to hit
a Whig or a Whig to hit a Tory, under whatever literary guise he appeared. If the new
writer was not orthodox in the view of his
political or theological critic, he was not to
be tolerated as poet or historian. Dr. Johnson had said everything he could say against
an author when he declared that he was
a vile Whig. Macaulay, a Whig, always
consulted his prejudices for his judgment,
equally when he was reviewing Croker's
Boswell or the impeachment of Warren
Hastings. He hated Croker, — a hateful
man, to be sure, — and when the latter published his edition of Boswell, Macaulay saw
his opportunity, and exclaimed before he
had looked at the book, as you will remember, " Now I will dust his jacket." The
standard of criticism does not lie with the
individual in literature any more than it
does in different periods as to fashions and
manners. The world is pretty well agreed,

and always has been, as to the qualities that make a gentleman. And yet there was a time when the vilest and perhaps the most contemptible man who ever occupied the English throne, — and that is saying a great deal, — George IV, was universally called the "First Gentleman of Europe." The reproach might be somewhat lightened by the fact that George was a foreigner, but for the wider fact that no person of English stock has been on the throne since Saxon Harold, the chosen and imposed rulers of England having been French, Welsh, Scotch, and Dutch, many of them being guiltless of the English language, and many of them also of the English middle-class morality. The impartial old Wraxall, the memorialist of the times of George III, having described a noble as a gambler, a drunkard, a smuggler, an appropriator of public money, who always cheated his tradesmen, who was one and sometimes all of them together, and a profligate generally, commonly adds, "But he was a perfect gentleman." And yet there has always been a standard that excludes

George IV from the rank of gentleman, as it excludes Tupper from the rank of poet.

The standard of literary judgment, then, is not in the individual, — that is, in the taste and prejudice of the individual, — any more than it is in the immediate contemporary opinion, which is always in flux and reflux from one extreme to another; but it is in certain immutable principles and qualities which have been slowly evolved during the long historic periods of literary criticism. But how shall we ascertain what these principles are, so as to apply them to new circumstances and new creations, holding on to the essentials and disregarding contemporary tastes, prejudices, and appearances? We all admit that certain pieces of literature have become classic; by general consent there is no dispute about them. How they have become so we cannot exactly explain. Some say by a mysterious settling of universal opinion, the operation of which cannot be exactly defined. Others say that the highly developed critical judgment of a few persons, from time to time, has established forever what we agree to call masterpieces. But this discussion is immaterial, since these supreme examples of literary excellence exist in all kinds of composition, — poetry, fable, romance, ethical teaching, prophecy, interpretation, history, humor, satire, devotional flight into the spiritual and supernatural, everything in which the human mind has exercised itself, — from the days of the Egyptian moralist and the Old Testament annalist and poet down to our scientific age. These masterpieces exist from many periods and in many languages, and they all have qualities in common which have insured their persistence.

To discover what these qualities are that have insured permanence and promise indefinite continuance is to have a means of judging with an approach to scientific accuracy our contemporary literature. There is no thing of beauty that does not conform to a law of order and beauty — poem, story, costume, picture, statue, all fall into an ascertainable law of art. Nothing of man's mak-

2   [17]

ing is perfect, but any creation approximates perfection in the measure that it conforms to inevitable law. To ascertain this law, and apply it, in art or in literature, to the changing conditions of our progressive life, is the business of the artist. It is the business of the critic to mark how the performance conforms to or departs from the law evolved and transmitted in the long experience of the race. True criticism, then, is not a matter of caprice or of individual liking or disliking, nor of conformity to a prevailing and generally temporary popular judgment. Individual judgment may be very interesting and have its value, depending upon the capacity of the judge. It was my good fortune once to fall in with a person who had been moved, by I know not what inspiration, to project himself out of his safe local conditions into France, Greece, Italy, Cairo, and Jerusalem. He assured me that he had seen nothing anywhere in the wide world of nature and art to compare with the beauty of Nebraska.

What are the qualities common to all the masterpieces of literature, or, let us say, to those that have endured in spite of imperfections and local provincialisms?

First of all I should name simplicity, which includes lucidity of expression, the clear thought in fitting, luminous words. And this is true when the thought is profound and the subject is as complex as life itself. This quality is strikingly exhibited for us in Jowett's translation of Plato, — which is as modern in feeling and phrase as anything done in Boston, — in the naïf and direct Herodotus, and, above all, in the King James vernacular translation of the Bible, which is the great text-book of all modern literature.

The second quality is knowledge of human nature. We can put up with the improbable in invention, because the improbable is always happening in life, but we cannot tolerate the so-called psychological juggling with the human mind, the perversion of the laws of the mind, the forcing of character to fit the eccentricities of plot. Whatever excursions the writer makes in fancy, we require fundamental consistency with human nature. And this is the reason why psychological studies of the abnormal, or biographies of criminal lunatics are only interesting to pathologists and never become classics in literature.

A third quality common to all master-pieces is what we call charm, a matter more or less of style, and which may be defined as the agreeable personality of the writer. This is indispensable. It is this personality which gives the final value to every work of art as well as of literature. It is not enough to copy nature or to copy, even accurately, the incidents of life. Only by digestion and transmutation through personality does any work attain the dignity of art. The great works of architecture, even, which are some-what determined by mathematical rule, owe their charm to the personal genius of their creators. For this reason our imitations of Greek architecture are commonly failures. To speak technically, the masterpiece of literature is characterised by the same knowl-edge of proportion and perspective as the masterpiece in art.

If there is a standard of literary excellence,

as there is a law of beauty, — and it seems
to me that to doubt this in the intellectual
world is to doubt the prevalence of order that
exists in the natural, — it is certainly possible
to ascertain whether a new production conforms, and how far it conforms, to the universally accepted canons of art. To work
by this rule in literary criticism is to substitute something definite for the individual
tastes, moods, and local bias of the critic. It
is true that the vast body of that which we
read is ephemeral, and justifies its existence
by its obvious use for information, recreation,
and entertainment. But to permit the impression to prevail that an unenlightened
popular preference for a book, however many
may hold it, is to be taken as a measure of
its excellence, is like claiming that a debased
Austrian coin, because it circulates, is as good
as a gold stater of Alexander. The case is
infinitely worse than this; for a slovenly
literature, unrebuked and uncorrected, begets
slovenly thought and debases our entire intellectual life.

It should be remembered, however, that

the creative faculty in man has not ceased, nor has puny man drawn all there is to be drawn out of the eternal wisdom. We are probably only in the beginning of our evolution, and something new may always be expected, that is, new and fresh applications of universal law. The critic of literature needs to be in an expectant and receptive frame of mind. Many critics approach a book with hostile intent, and seem to fancy that their business is to look for what is bad in it, and not for what is good. It seems to me that the first duty of the critic is to try to understand the author, to give him a fair chance by coming to his perusal with an open mind. Whatever book you read, or sermon or lecture you hear, give yourself for the time absolutely to its influence. This is just to the author, fair to the public, and, above all, valuable to the intellectual sanity of the critic himself. It is a very bad thing for the memory and the judgment to get into a habit of reading carelessly or listening with distracted attention. I know of nothing so harmful to the strength of the mind as this habit. There

is a valuable mental training in closely following a discourse that is valueless in itself.
After the reader has unreservedly surrendered himself to the influence of a book, and
let his mind settle, as we say, and resume its
own judgment, he is in a position to look at
it objectively and to compare it with other
facts of life and of literature dispassionately.
He can then compare it as to form, substance,
tone, with the enduring literature that has
come down to us from all the ages. It is a
phenomenon known to all of us that we may
for the moment be carried away by a book
which upon cool reflection we find is false in
ethics and weak in construction. We find
this because we have standards outside ourselves.

I am not concerned to define here what is
meant by literature. A great mass of it has
been accumulated in the progress of mankind,
and, fortunately for different wants and tem-
peraments, it is as varied as the various minds
that produced it. The main thing to be considered is that this great stream of thought
is the highest achievement and the most

valuable possession of mankind. It is not only that literature is the source of inspiration to youth and the solace of age, but it is what a national language is to a nation, the highest expression of its being. Whatever we acquire of science, of art, in discovery, in the application of natural laws in industries, is an enlargement of our horizon, and a contribution to the highest needs of man, his intellectual life. The controversy between the claims of the practical life and the intellectual is as idle as the so-called conflict between science and religion. And the highest and final expression of this life of man, his thought, his emotion, his feeling, his aspiration, whatever you choose to call it, is in the enduring literature he creates. He certainly misses half his opportunity on this planet who considers only the physical or what is called the practical. He is a man only half developed. I can conceive no more dreary existence than that of a man who is past the period of business activity, and who cannot, for his entertainment, his happiness, draw upon the great reservoir of literature. For

what did I come into this world if I am
to be like a stake planted in a fence, and not
like a tree visited by all the winds of heaven
and the birds of the air?

Those who concern themselves with the
printed matter in books and periodicals are
often in despair over the volume of it, and
their actual inability to keep up with current literature. They need not worry. If all
that appears in books, under the pressure of
publishers and the ambition of experimenters
in writing, were uniformly excellent, no reader
would be under any more obligation to read
it than he is to see every individual flower
and blossoming shrub. Specimens of the
varieties would suffice. But a vast proportion of it is the product of immature minds,
and of a yearning for experience rather than
a knowledge of life. There is no more obligation on the part of the person who would
be well informed and cultivated to read all
this than there is to read all the coloured incidents, personal gossip, accidents, and crimes
repeated daily, with sameness of effect, in the
newspapers, some of the most widely circu-

lated of which are a composite of the police
gazette and the comic almanac. A great deal
of the reading done is mere contagion, one
form or another of communicated grippe,
and it is consoling and even surprising to
know that if you escape the run of it for a
season, you have lost nothing appreciable.
Some people, it has been often said, make it
a rule never to read a book until it is from
one to five years old. By this simple device
they escape the necessity of reading most of
them, but this is only a part of their gain.
Considering the fact that the world is full of
books of the highest value for cultivation,
entertainment, and information, which the
utmost leisure we can spare from other
pressing avocations does not suffice to give
us knowledge of, it does seem to be little
less than a moral and intellectual sin to
flounder about blindly in the flood of new
publications. I am speaking, of course, of
the general mass of readers, and not of the
specialists who must follow their subjects
with ceaseless inquisition. But for most of
us who belong to the still comparatively few

who really read books, the main object of life is not to keep up with the printing-press, any more than it is the main object of sensible people to follow all the extremes and whims of fashion in dress. When a fashion in literature has passed, we are surprised that it should ever have seemed worth the trouble of studying or imitating. When the special craze has passed, we notice another thing, and that is that the author, not being of the first rank or of the second, has generally contributed to the world all that he has to give in one book, and our time has been wasted on his other books; and also that in a special kind of writing in a given period — let us say, for example, the historico-romantic — we perceive that it all has a common character, is constructed on the same lines of adventure and with a prevailing type of hero and heroine, according to the pattern set by the first one or two stories of the sort which became popular, and we see its more or less mechanical construction, and how easily it degenerates into commercial book-making. Now while some of this writing has an individual flavour that makes it entertaining and profitable in this way, we may be excused from attempting to follow it all merely because it happens to be talked about for the moment, and generally talked about in a very undiscriminating manner. We need not in any company be ashamed if we have not read it all, especially if we are ashamed that, considering the time at our disposal, we have not made the acquaintance of the great and small masterpieces of literature. It is said that the fashion of this world passeth away, and so does the mere fashion in literature, the fashion that does not follow the eternal law of beauty and symmetry, and contribute to the intellectual and spiritual part of man. Otherwise it is only a waiting in a material existence, like the lovers, in the words of the Arabian story-teller, "till there came to them the Destroyer of Delights and the Sunderer of Companies, he who layeth waste the palaces and peopleth the tombs."

Without special anxiety, then, to keep pace with all the ephemeral in literature, lest we should miss for the moment something that is permanent, we can rest content in the vast accumulation of the tried and genuine that the ages have given us. Anything that really belongs to literature to-day we shall certainly find awaiting us to-morrow.

The better part of the life of man is in and by the imagination. This is not generally believed, because it is not generally believed that the chief end of man is the accumulation of intellectual and spiritual material. Hence it is that what is called a practical education is set above the mere enlargement and enrichment of the mind; and the possession of the material is valued, and the intellectual life is undervalued. But it should be remembered that the best preparation for a practical and useful life is in the high development of the powers of the mind, and that, commonly, by a culture that is not considered practical. The notable fact about the group of great parliamentary orators in the days of George III is the exhibition of their intellectual resources in the entire world of letters, the classics, and ancient and modern history. Yet all of them owed

[29]

their development to a strictly classical training in the schools. And most of them had not only the gift of the imagination necessary to great eloquence, but also were so mentally disciplined by the classics that they handled the practical questions upon which they legislated with clearness and precision. The great masters of finance were the classically trained orators William Pitt and Charles James Fox.

In fine, to return to our knowledge of the short life of fashions that are for the moment striking, why should we waste precious time in chasing meteoric appearances, when we can be warmed and invigorated in the sunshine of the great literatures?

The American Newspaper

OUR theme for the hour is the American Newspaper. It is a subject in which everybody is interested, and about which it is not polite to say that anybody is not well informed; for, although there are scattered through the land many persons, I am sorry to say, unable to pay for a newspaper, I have never yet heard of anybody unable to edit one.

The topic has many points of view, and invites various study and comment. In our limited time we must select one only. We have heard a great deal about the power, the opportunity, the duty, the "mission," of the press. The time has come for a more philosophical treatment of it, for an inquiry into its relations to our complex civilisation, for some ethical account of it as one of the developments of our day, and for some discussion of the effect it is producing, and likely to produce, on the education of the people. Has the time come, or is it near at hand, when we can point to a person who is alert, superficial, ready and shallow, self-confident and half-informed, and say, " There is a product of the American newspaper"? The newspaper is not a wilful creation, nor an isolated phenomenon, but the legitimate outcome of our age, as much as our system of popular education. And I trust that some competent observer will make, perhaps for this association, a philosophical study of it. My task here is a much humbler one. I have thought that it may not be unprofitable to treat the newspaper from a practical and even somewhat mechanical point of view.

The newspaper is a private enterprise. Its object is to make money for its owner. Whatever motive may be given out for starting a newspaper, expectation of profit by it is the real one, whether the newspaper is religious, political, scientific, or literary. The exceptional cases of newspapers devoted to ideas or "causes" without regard to profit are so few as not to affect the rule. Commonly, the cause, the sect, the party, the trade, the delusion, the idea, gets its newspaper, its organ, its advocate, only when some individual thinks he can see a pecuniary return in establishing it.

This motive is not lower than that which leads people into any other occupation or profession. To make a living, and to have a career, is the original incentive in all cases. Even in purely philanthropical enterprises the driving-wheel that keeps them in motion for any length of time is the salary paid the working members. So powerful is this incentive, that sometimes the wheel will continue to turn round when there is no grist to grind. It sometimes happens that the friction of the philanthropic machinery is so great, that but very little power is transmitted to the object for which the machinery was made. I knew a devoted agent of the American Colonisation Society, who, for several years, collected in Connecticut just enough, for the cause, to buy his clothes, and pay his board at a good hotel.

It is scarcely necessary to say, except to

prevent a possible misapprehension, that the editor who has no high ideals, no intention of benefiting his fellow-men by his newspaper, and uses it unscrupulously as a means of money-making only, sinks to the level of the physician and the lawyer who have no higher conception of their callings than that they offer opportunities for getting money by appeals to credulity, and by assisting in evasions of the law.

If the excellence of a newspaper is not always measured by its profitableness, it is generally true, that, if it does not pay its owner, it is valueless to the public. Not all newspapers which make money are good, for some succeed by catering to the lowest tastes of respectable people, and to the prejudice, ignorance, and passion of the lowest class; but, as a rule, the successful journal pecuniarily is the best journal. The reasons for this are on the surface. The impecunious newspaper cannot give its readers promptly the news, nor able discussion of the news, and, still worse, it cannot be independent. The political journal that relies for support upon drippings of party favour or patronage, the general newspaper that finds it necessary to existence to manipulate stock reports, the religious weekly that draws precarious support from puffing doubtful enterprises, the literary paper that depends upon the approval of publishers, are poor affairs, and, in the long run or short run, come to grief. Some newspapers do succeed by sensationalism, as some preachers do; by a kind of quackery, as some doctors do; by trimming and shifting to any momentary popular prejudice, as some politicians do; by becoming the paid advocate of a personal ambition or a corporate enterprise, as some lawyers do: but the newspaper only becomes a real power when it is able, on the basis of pecuniary independence, to free itself from all such entanglements. An editor who stands with hat in hand has the respect accorded to any other beggar.

The recognition of the fact that the newspaper is a private and purely business enterprise will help to define the mutual relations of the editor and the public. His claim upon the public is exactly that of any manufacturer or dealer. It is that of the man who makes cloth, or the grocer who opens a shop : neither has a right to complain if the public does not buy of him. If the buyer does not like a cloth half shoddy, or coffee half chicory, he will go elsewhere. If the subscriber does not like one newspaper, he takes another, or none. The appeal for newspaper support on the ground that such a journal ought to be sustained by an enlightened community, or on any other ground than that it is a good article that people want, — or would want if they knew its value, — is purely childish in this age of the world. If any person wants to start a periodical devoted to decorated teapots, with the noble view of inducing the people to live up to his idea of a teapot, very good ; but he has no right to complain if he fails.

On the other hand, the public has no rights in the newspaper except what it pays for; even the "old subscriber" has none, except to drop the paper if it ceases to please him. The notion that the subscriber has a right to interfere in the conduct of the paper, or the reader to direct its opinions, is based

on a misconception of what the newspaper is.
The claim of the public to have its communi-
cations printed in the paper is equally baseless. Whether they shall be printed or not
rests in the discretion of the editor, having
reference to his own private interest, and to
his apprehension of the public good. Nor
is he bound to give any reason for his refusal. It is purely in his discretion whether
he will admit a reply to anything that has
appeared in his columns. No one has a
right to demand it. Courtesy and policy
may grant it; but the right to it does not
exist. If any one is injured, he may seek his
remedy at law; and I should like to see
the law of libel such and so administered
that any person injured by a libel in the
newspaper, as well as by slander out of it,
could be sure of prompt redress. While the
subscriber acquires no right to dictate to the
newspaper, we can imagine an extreme case
when he should have his money back which
had been paid in advance, if the newspaper
totally changed its character. If he had
contracted with a dealer to supply him with

hard coal during the winter, he might have a remedy if the dealer delivered only charcoal in the coldest weather; and so if he paid for a Roman-Catholic journal which suddenly became an organ of the spiritists.

The advertiser acquires no more rights in the newspaper than the subscriber. He is entitled to use the space for which he pays by the insertion of such material as is approved by the editor. He gains no interest in any other part of the paper, and has no more claim to any space in the editorial columns, than any other one of the public. To give him such space would be unbusiness-like, and the extension of a preference which would be unjust to the rest of the public. Nothing more quickly destroys the character of a journal, begets distrust of it, and so reduces its value, than the well-founded suspicion that its editorial columns are the property of advertisers. Even a religious journal will, after a while, be injured by this.

Yet it must be confessed that here is one of the greatest difficulties of modern

journalism. The newspaper must be cheap.
It is, considering the immense cost to produce it, the cheapest product ever offered to
man. Most newspapers cost more than they
sell for; they could not live by subscriptions;
for any profits, they certainly depend upon
advertisements. The advertisements depend
upon the circulation; the circulation is likely
to dwindle if too much space is occupied by
advertisements, or if it is evident that the
paper belongs to its favoured advertisers.
The counting-room desires to conciliate the
advertisers; the editor looks to making a
paper satisfactory to his readers. Between
this see-saw of the necessary subscriber and
the necessary advertiser, a good many newspapers go down. This difficulty would be
measurably removed by the admission of the
truth that the newspaper is a strictly business enterprise, depending for success upon
a *quid pro quo* between all parties con-
nected with it, and upon integrity in its
management.

Akin to the false notion that the newspaper is a sort of open channel that the

public may use as it chooses, is the conception of it as a charitable institution. The newspaper, which is the property of a private person as much as a drug-shop is, is expected to perform for nothing services which would be asked of no other private person. There is scarcely a charitable enterprise to which it is not asked to contribute of its space, which is money, ten times more than other persons in the community, who are ten times as able as the owner of the newspaper, contribute. The journal is considered "mean" if it will not surrender its columns freely to notices and announcements of this sort. If a manager has a new hen-coop or a new singer he wishes to introduce to the public, he comes to the newspaper, expecting to have his enterprise extolled for nothing, and probably never thinks that it would be just as proper for him to go to one of the regular advertisers in the paper and ask him to give up his space. Anything, from a church picnic to a brass-band concert for the benefit of the widow of the triangles, asks the newspaper to contribute. The party in politics, whose principles the editor advocates, has no doubt of its rightful claim upon him, not only upon the editorial columns, but upon the whole newspaper. It asks without hesitation that the newspaper should take up its valuable space by printing hundreds and often thousands of dollars' worth of political announcements in the course of a protracted campaign, when it never would think of getting its halls, its speakers, and its brass bands, free of expense. Churches, as well as parties, expect this sort of charity. I have known rich churches, to whose members it was a convenience to have their Sunday and other services announced, withdraw the announcements when the editor declined any longer to contribute a weekly fifty-cents' worth of space. No private persons contribute so much to charity, in proportion to ability, as the newspaper. Perhaps it will get credit for this in the next world: it certainly never does in this.

The chief function of the newspaper is to collect and print the news. Upon the kind of news that should be gathered and published, we shall remark farther on. The second function is to elucidate the news, and comment on it, and show its relations. A third function is to furnish reading-matter to the general public.

Nothing is so difficult for the manager as to know what news is: the instinct for it is a sort of sixth sense. To discern out of the mass of materials collected not only what is most likely to interest the public, but what phase and aspect of it will attract most attention, and the relative importance of it; to tell the day before or at midnight what the world will be talking about in the morning, and what it will want the fullest details of, and to meet that want in advance, — requires a peculiar talent. There is always some topic on which the public wants instant information. It is easy enough when the news is developed, and everybody is discussing it, for the editor to fall in; but the success of the news printed depends upon a pre-apprehension of all this. Some papers, which nevertheless print all the news, are always a day behind, do not appreciate the popular drift till it has gone to something else, and err as much by clinging to a subject after it is dead as by not taking it up before it was fairly born. The public craves eagerly for only one thing at a time, and soon wearies of that; and it is to the newspaper's profit to seize the exact point of a debate, the thrilling moment of an accident, the pith of an important discourse; to throw itself into it as if life depended on it, and for the hour to flood the popular curiosity with it as an engine deluges a fire.

Scarcely less important than promptly seizing and printing the news is the attractive arrangement of it, its effective presentation to the eye. Two papers may have exactly the same important intelligence, identically the same despatches: the one will be called bright, attractive, "newsy;" the other, dull and stupid.

We have said nothing yet about that, which, to most people, is the most important aspect of the newspaper, — the editor's responsibility to the public for its contents. It is sufficient briefly to say here, that it is exactly the responsibility of every other person in society, — the full responsibility of his opportunity. He has voluntarily taken a position in which he can do a great deal of good or a great deal of evil, and he should be held and judged by his opportunity: it is greater than that of the preacher, the teacher, the congressman, the physician. He occupies the loftiest pulpit; he is in his teacher's desk seven days in the week; his voice can be heard farther than that of the most lusty fog-horn politician; and often, I am sorry to say, his columns outshine the shelves of the druggist in display of proprietary medicines. Nothing else ever invented has the public attention as the newspaper has, or is an influence so constant and universal. It is this large opportunity that has given the impression that the newspaper is a public rather than a private enterprise.

It was a nebulous but suggestive remark that the newspaper occupies the borderland between literature and common sense. Literature it certainly is not, and in the popular apprehension it seems often too erratic and variable to be credited with the balance-wheel of sense; but it must have something of the charm of the one, and the steadiness and sagacity of the other, or it will fail to please. The model editor, I believe, has yet to appear. Notwithstanding the traditional reputation of certain editors in the past, they could not be called great editors by our standards; for the elements of modern journalism did not exist in their time. The old newspaper was a broadside of stale news, with a moral essay attached. Perhaps Benjamin Franklin, with our facilities, would have been very near the ideal editor. There was nothing he did not wish to know; and no one excelled him in the ability to communicate what he found out to the average mind. He came as near as anybody ever did to marrying common sense to literature: he had it in him to make it sufficient for journalistic purposes. He was what somebody said Carlyle was, and what the American editor ought to be, — a vernacular man.

The assertion has been made recently, publicly, and with evidence adduced, that the American newspaper is the best in the world. It is like the assertion that the American government is the best in the world; no doubt it is, for the American people.

Judged by broad standards, it may safely be admitted that the American newspaper is susceptible of some improvement, and that it has something to learn from the journals of other nations. We shall be better employed in correcting its weaknesses than in complacently contemplating its excellences.

Let us examine it in its three departments already named, — its news, editorials, and miscellaneous reading-matter.

In particularity and comprehensiveness of news-collecting, it may be admitted that the American newspapers for a time led the world. I mean in the picking-up of local intelligence, and the use of the telegraph to make it general. And with this arose the odd notion that news is made important by the mere fact of its rapid transmission over the wire. The English journals followed, speedily overtook, and some of the wealthier ones perhaps surpassed, the American in the use of the telegraph, and in the presentation of some sorts of local news; not of casualties, and small city and neighbourhood events, and social gossip (until very recently), but certainly in the business of the law courts, and the crimes and mishaps that come within police and legal supervision. The leading papers of the German press, though strong in correspondence and in discussion of affairs, are far less comprehensive in their news than the American or the English. The French journals, we are accustomed to say, are not newspapers at all. And this is true as we use the word. Until recently, nothing has been of importance to the Frenchman except himself; and what happened outside of France, not directly affecting his glory, his profit, or his pleasure, did not interest him: hence, one could nowhere so securely intrench himself against the news of the world as behind the barricade of the Paris journals. But let us not make a mistake in this matter. We may have more to learn from the Paris journals than from any

[47]

others. If they do not give what we call news — local news, events, casualties, the happenings of the day, — they do give ideas, opinions; they do discuss politics, the social drift; they give the intellectual ferment of Paris; they supply the material that Paris likes to talk over, the badinage of the boulevard, the wit of the salon, the sensation of the stage, the new movement in literature and in politics. This may be important, or it may be trivial: it is commonly more interesting than much of that which we call news.

Our very facility and enterprise in news-gathering have overwhelmed our newspapers, and it may be remarked that editorial discrimination has not kept pace with the facilities. We are overpowered with a mass of undigested intelligence, collected for the most part without regard to value. The force of the newspaper is expended in extending these facilities, with little regard to discriminating selection. The burden is already too heavy for the newspaper, and wearisome to the public.

The publication of the news is the most important function of the paper. How is it gathered? We must confess that it is gathered very much by chance. A drag-net is thrown out, and whatever comes is taken. An examination into the process of collecting shows what sort of news we are likely to get, and that nine-tenths of that printed is collected without much intelligence exercised in selection. The alliance of the associated press with the telegraph company is a fruitful source of news of an inferior quality. Of course, it is for the interest of the telegraph company to swell the volume to be transmitted. It is impossible for the associated press to have an agent in every place to which the telegraph penetrates: therefore the telegraphic operators often act as its purveyors. It is for their interest to send something; and their judgment of what is important is not only biassed, but is formed by purely local standards. Our news, therefore, is largely set in motion by telegraphic operators, by agents trained to regard only the accidental, the startling, the

4 [49]

abnormal, as news; it is picked up by sharp prowlers about town, whose pay depends upon finding something, who are looking for something spicy and sensational, or which may be dressed up and exaggerated to satisfy an appetite for novelty and high flavour, and who regard casualties as the chief news. Our newspapers every day are loaded with accidents, casualties, and crimes concerning people of whom we never heard before and never shall hear again, the reading of which is of no earthly use to any human being.

What is news? What is it that an intelligent public should care to hear of and talk about? Run your eye down the columns of your journal. There was a drunken squabble last night in a New York groggery; there is a petty but carefully elaborated village scandal about a foolish girl; a woman accidentally dropped her baby out of a fourth-story window in Maine; in Connecticut, a wife, by mistake, got into the same railway train with another woman's husband; a child fell into a well in New Jersey; there is a column about a peripatetic horse-race, which exhibits,

like a circus, from city to city; a labourer in
a remote town in Pennsylvania had a sun-
stroke; there is an edifying dying speech of
a murderer, the love-letter of a suicide, the
set-to of a couple of congressmen; and there
are columns about the gigantic war of half a
dozen politicians over the appointment of a
sugar-gauger. Granted that this pabulum
is desired by the reader, why not save the
expense of transmission by having several
columns of it stereotyped, to be reproduced
at proper intervals? With the date changed,
it would always have its original value, and
perfectly satisfy the demand, if a demand exists, for this sort of news.

This is not, as you see, a description of
your journal: it is a description of only one
portion of it. It is a complex and wonderful
creation. Every morning it is a mirror of
the world, more or less distorted and imper-
fect, but such a mirror as it never had held
up to it before. But consider how much
space is taken up with mere trivialities and
vulgarities under the name of news. And
this evil is likely to continue and increase

until news-gatherers learn that more important than the reports of accidents and casualties is the intelligence of opinions and thoughts, the moral and intellectual movements of modern life. A horrible assassination in India is instantly telegraphed; but the progress of such a vast movement as that of the Wahabee revival in Islam, which may change the destiny of great provinces, never gets itself put upon the wires. We hear promptly of a land-slide in Switzerland, but only very slowly of a political agitation that is changing the constitution of the republic. It should be said, however, that the daily newspaper is not alone responsible for this: it is what the age and the community where it is published make it. So far as I have observed, the majority of the readers in America peruses eagerly three columns about a mill between an English and a naturalised American prize-fighter, but will only glance at a column report of a debate in the English parliament which involves a radical change in the whole policy of England; and devours a page about the Chantilly races,

[52]

while it ignores a paragraph concerning the suppression of the Jesuit schools.

Our newspapers are overwhelmed with material that is of no importance. The obvious remedy for this would be more intelligent direction in the collection of news, and more careful sifting and supervision of it when gathered. It becomes every day more apparent to every manager that such discrimination is more necessary. There is no limit to the various intelligence and gossip that our complex life offers: no paper is big enough to contain it; no reader has time enough to read it. And the journal must cease to be a sort of waste-basket at the end of a telegraph wire, into which any reporter, telegraph operator, or gossip-monger can dump whatever he pleases. We must get rid of the superstition that value is given to an unimportant " item " by sending it a thousand miles over a wire.

Perhaps the most striking feature of the American newspaper, especially of the country weekly, is its enormous development of local and neighbourhood news. It is of

recent date. Horace Greeley used to advise
the country editors to give small space to
the general news of the world, but to cultivate assiduously the home field, to glean
every possible detail of private life in the
circuit of the county, and print it. The
advice was shrewd for a metropolitan editor,
and it was not without its profit to the country editor. It was founded on a deep knowledge of human nature; namely, upon the
fact that people read most eagerly that
which they already know, if it is about themselves or their neighbours, if it is a report
of something they have been concerned in,
a lecture they have heard, a fair, or festival,
or wedding, or funeral, or barn-raising they
have attended. The result is column after
column of short paragraphs of gossip and
trivialities, chips, chips, chips. Mr. Sales is
contemplating erecting a new counter in his
store; his rival opposite has a new sign;
Miss Bumps of Gath is visiting her cousin,
Miss Smith of Bozrah; the sheriff has
painted his fence; Farmer Brown has lost
his cow; the eminent member from Neopo-

lis has put an ell on one end of his mansion, and a mortgage on the other.

On the face of it nothing is so vapid and profitless as column after column of this reading. These "items" have very little interest, except to those who already know the facts; but those concerned like to see them in print, and take the newspaper on that account. This sort of inanity takes the place of reading-matter that might be of benefit, and its effect must be to belittle and contract the mind. But this is not the most serious objection to the publication of these worthless details. It cultivates self-consciousness in the community, and love of notoriety; it develops vanity and self-importance, and elevates the trivial in life above the essential.

And this brings me to speak of the mania in this age, and especially in America, for notoriety in social life as well as in politics. The newspapers are the vehicle of it, sometimes the occasion, but not the cause. The newspaper may have fostered — it has not created — this hunger for publicity. Almost everybody talks about the violation of decency and the sanctity of private life by the newspaper in the publication of personalities and the gossip of society; and the very people who make these strictures are often those who regard the paper as without enterprise and dull, if it does not report in detail their weddings, their balls and parties, the distinguished persons present, the dress of the ladies, the sumptuousness of the entertainment, if it does not celebrate their church services and festivities, their social meetings, their new house, their distinguished arrivals at this or that watering-place. I believe every newspaper manager will bear me out in saying that there is a constant pressure on him to print much more of such private matter than his judgment and taste permit or approve, and that the gossip which is brought to his notice, with the hope that he will violate the sensitiveness of social life by printing it, is far away larger in amount than all that he publishes.

To return for a moment to the subject of

general news. The characteristic of our modern civilisation is sensitiveness, or, as the doctors say, nervousness. Perhaps the philanthropist would term it sympathy. No doubt an exciting cause of it is the adaptation of electricity to the transmission of facts and ideas. The telegraph, we say, has put us in sympathy with all the world. And we reckon this enlargement of nerve contact somehow a gain. Our bared nerves are played upon by a thousand wires. Nature, no doubt, has a method of hardening or deadening them to these shocks; but, nevertheless, every person who reads is a focus for the excitements, the ills, the troubles, of all the world. In addition to his local pleasures and annoyances, he is in a manner compelled to be a sharer in the universal uneasiness. It might be worth while to inquire what effect this exciting accumulation of the news of the world upon an individual or a community has upon happiness and upon character. Is the New-England man any better able to bear or deal with his extraordinary climate by the daily knowledge of the weather all over the globe? Is a man happier, or improved in character, by the woful tale of a world's distress and apprehension that greets him every morning at breakfast? Knowledge, we know, increases sorrow; but I suppose the offset to that is, that strength only comes through suffering. But this is a digression.

Not second in importance to any department of the journal is the reporting; that is, the special reporting as distinguished from the more general news-gathering. I mean the reports of proceedings in Congress, in conventions, assemblies, and conferences, public conversations, lectures, sermons, investigations, law trials, and occurrences of all sorts that rise into general importance. These reports are the basis of our knowledge and opinions. If they are false or exaggerated, we are ignorant of what is taking place, and misled. It is of infinitely more importance that they should be absolutely trustworthy than that the editorial comments should be sound and wise. If the reports on affairs can be depended on, the public can form its own opinion, and act intelligently. And, if the public has a right to demand anything of a newspaper, it is that its reports of what occurs shall be faithfully accurate, unprejudiced, and colourless. They ought not to be editorials, or the vehicles of personal opinion and feeling. The interpretation of the facts they give should be left to the editor and the public. There should be a sharp line drawn between the report and the editorial.

I am inclined to think that the reporting department is the weakest in the American newspaper, and that there is just ground for the admitted public distrust of it. Too often, if a person would know what has taken place in a given case, he must read the reports in half a dozen journals, then strike a general average of probabilities, allowing for the personal equation, and then — suspend his judgment. Of course, there is much excellent reporting, and there are many able men engaged in it who reflect the highest honour upon their occupation. And the press of no other country shows

more occasional brilliant feats in reporting
than ours : these are on occasions when the
newspapers make special efforts. Take the
last two national party conventions. The
fulness, the accuracy, the vividness, with
which their proceedings were reported in the
leading journals, were marvellous triumphs
of knowledge, skill, and expense. The conventions were so photographed by hundreds
of pens, that the public outside saw them
almost as distinctly as the crowd in attendance. This result was attained because the
editors determined that it should be, sent
able men to report, and demanded the best
work. But take an opposite and a daily illustration of reporting, that of the debates and
proceedings in Congress. I do not refer to
the specials of various journals which are
good, bad, or indifferent, as the case may
be, and commonly coloured by partisan considerations, but the regular synopsis sent
to the country at large. Now, for some
years it has been inadequate, frequently unintelligible, often grossly misleading, failing
wholly to give the real spirit and meaning

of the most important discussions; and it is as dry as chips besides. To be both stupid and inaccurate is the unpardonable sin in journalism. Contrast these reports with the lively and faithful pictures of the French Assembly which are served to the Paris papers.

Before speaking of the reasons for the public distrust in reports, it is proper to put in one qualification. The public itself, and not the newspapers, is the great factory of baseless rumours and untruths. Although the newspaper unavoidably gives currency to some of these, it is the great corrector of popular rumours. Concerning any event, a hundred different versions and conflicting accounts are instantly set afloat. These would run on, and become settled but unfounded beliefs, as private whispered scandals do run, if the newspaper did not intervene. It is the business of the newspaper, on every occurrence of moment, to chase down the rumours, and to find out the facts and print them, and set the public mind at rest. The newspaper publishes them under a sense of responsibility for its statements. It is not by any means always correct; but I know that it is the aim of most newspapers to discharge this important public function faithfully. When this country had few newspapers it was ten times more the prey of false reports and delusions than it is now.

Reporting requires as high ability as editorial writing; perhaps of a different kind, though in the history of American journalism the best reporters have often become the best editors. Talent of this kind must be adequately paid; and it happens that in America the reporting field is so vast that few journals can afford to make the reporting department correspond in ability to the editorial, and I doubt if the importance of doing so is yet fully realised. An intelligent and representative synopsis of a lecture or other public performance is rare. The ability to grasp a speaker's meaning, or to follow a long discourse, and reproduce either in spirit, and fairly, in a short space, is not common.

When the public which has been present reads the inaccurate report, it loses confidence in the newspaper.

Its confidence is again undermined when it learns that an "interview" which it has read with interest was manufactured; that the report of the movements and sayings of a distinguished stranger was a pure piece of ingenious invention; that a thrilling adventure alongshore, or in a balloon, or in a horse-car, was what is called a sensational article, concocted by some brilliant genius, and spun out by the yard according to his necessities. These reports are entertaining, and often more readable than anything else in the newspaper; and, if they were put into a department with an appropriate heading, the public would be less suspicious that all the news in the journal was coloured and heightened by a lively imagination.

Intelligent and honest reporting of whatever interests the public is the sound basis of all journalism. And yet so careless have editors been of all this, that a reporter has been sent to attend the sessions of a philological convention who had not the least linguistic knowledge, having always been employed on marine disasters. Another reporter, who was assigned to inform the public of the results of a difficult archæological investigation, frankly confessed his inability to understand what was going on; for his ordinary business, he said, was cattle. A story is told of a metropolitan journal, which illustrates another difficulty the public has in keeping up its confidence in newspaper infallibility. It may not be true for history, but answers for an illustration. The annual November meteors were expected on a certain night. The journal prepared an elaborate article, several columns in length, on meteoric displays in general, and on the display of that night in particular, giving in detail the appearance of the heavens from the metropolitan roofs in various parts of the city, the shooting of the meteors amid the blazing constellations, the size and times of flight of the fiery bodies; in short, a most vivid and scientific account of the lofty fireworks. Unfortunately the night was cloudy.

The article was in type and ready; but the clouds would not break. The last moment for going to press arrived: there was a probability that the clouds would lift before daylight and the manager took the risk. The article that appeared was very interesting; but its scientific value was impaired by the fact that the heavens were obscured the whole night, and the meteors, if any arrived, were invisible. The reasonable excuse of the editor would be that he could not control the elements.

If the reporting department needs strengthening and reduction to order in the American journal, we may also query whether the department of correspondence sustains the boast that the American newspaper is the best in the world. We have a good deal of excellent correspondence, both foreign and domestic; and our "specials" have won distinction, at least for liveliness and enterprise. I cannot dwell upon this feature; but I suggest a comparison with the correspondence of some of the German, and with that especially of the London journals, from the various capitals of Europe, and from the occasional seats of war. How surpassing able much of it is! How full of information, of philosophic observation, of accurate knowledge! It appears to be written by men of trained intellect and of experience, — educated men of the world, who, by reason of their position and character, have access to the highest sources of information.

The editorials of our journals seem to me better than formerly, improved in tone, in courtesy, in self-respect, — though you may not have to go far or search long for the provincial note and the easy grace of the frontier, — and they are better written. This is because the newspaper has become more profitable, and is able to pay for talent, and has attracted to it educated young men. There is a sort of editorial ability, of facility, of force, that can only be acquired by practice and in the newspaper office: no school can ever teach it; but the young editor who has a broad basis of general education, of information in history, political economy, the classics, and polite literature, has an immense advantage over the man who has merely practical experience. For the editorial, if it is to hold its place, must be more and more the product of information, culture, and reflection, as well as of sagacity and alertness. Ignorance of foreign affairs, and of economic science, the American people have in times past winked at; but they will not always wink at it.

It is the belief of some shrewd observers that editorials, the long editorials, are not much read, except by editors themselves. A cynic says, that, if you have a secret you are very anxious to keep from the female portion of the population, the safest place to put it is in an editorial. It seems to me that editorials are not conned as attentively as they once were; and I am sure they have not so much influence as formerly. People are not so easily or so visibly led; that is to say, the editorial influence is not so dogmatic and direct. The editor does not expect to form public opinion so much by arguments and appeals as by the news he presents and his manner of presenting it, by the iteration of

an idea until it becomes familiar, by the
reading-matter selected, and by the quota-
tions of opinions as news, and not professedly
to influence the reader. And this influence
is all the more potent because it is indirect,
and not perceived by the reader.

There is an editorial tradition — it might
almost be termed a superstition — which I
think will have to be abandoned. It is that
a certain space in the journal must be filled
with editorial, and that some of the editorials
must be long, without any reference to the
news or the necessity of comment on it, or
the capacity of the editor at the moment to
fill the space with original matter that is
readable. There is the sacred space, and it
must be filled. The London journals are
perfect types of this custom. The result is
often a wearisome page of words and rhetoric.
It may be good rhetoric; but life is too short
for so much of it. The necessity of filling
this space causes the writer, instead of stating
his idea in the shortest compass in which it
can be made perspicuous and telling, to beat
it out thin, and make it cover as much ground

as possible. This, also, is vanity. In the
economy of room, which our journals will
more and more be compelled to cultivate, I
venture to say that this tradition will be set
aside. I think that we may fairly claim a
superiority in our journals over the English
dailies in our habit of making brief, pointed
editorial paragraphs. They are the life of the
editorial page. A cultivation of these until
they are as finished and pregnant as the
paragraphs of "The London Spectator" and
"The New-York Nation," the printing of
long editorials only when the elucidation of
a subject demands length, and the use of the
space thus saved for more interesting reading, is probably the line of our editorial
evolution.

To continue the comparison of our journals as a class, with the English as a class,
ours are more lively, also more flippant, and
less restrained by a sense of responsibility or
by the laws of libel. We furnish, now and
again, as good editorial writing for its purpose; but it commonly lacks the dignity, the
thoroughness, the wide sweep and knowledge,

that characterises the best English discussion of political and social topics.

The third department of the newspaper is that of miscellaneous reading-matter. Whether this is the survival of the period when the paper contained little else except "selections," and other printed matter was scarce, or whether it is only the beginning of a development that shall supply the public nearly all its literature, I do not know. Far as our newspapers have already gone in this direction, I am inclined to think that in their evolution they must drop this adjunct, and print simply the news of the day. Some of the leading journals of the world already do this.

In America I am sure the papers are printing too much miscellaneous reading. The perusal of this smattering of everything, these scraps of information and snatches of literature, this infinite variety and medley, in which no subject is adequately treated, is distracting and debilitating to the mind. It prevents the reading of anything in full, and its satisfactory assimilation. It is said that the majority of Americans read nothing except the paper. If they read that thoroughly, they have time for nothing else. What is its reader to do when his journal thrusts upon him every day the amount contained in a fair-sized duodecimo volume, and on Sundays the amount of two of them? Granted that this miscellaneous hodge-podge is the cream of current literature, is it profitable to the reader? Is it a means of anything but superficial culture and fragmentary information? Besides, it stimulates an unnatural appetite, a liking for the striking, the brilliant, the sensational only; for our selections from current literature are usually the "plums;" and plums are not a wholesome diet for anybody. A person accustomed to this finds it difficult to sit down patiently to the mastery of a book or a subject, to the study of history, the perusal of extended biography, or to acquire that intellectual development and strength which comes from thorough reading and reflection.

The subject has another aspect. Nobody chooses his own reading; and a whole community perusing substantially the same material tends to a mental uniformity. The editor has the more than royal power of selecting the intellectual food of a large public. It is a responsibility infinitely greater than that of the compiler of schoolbooks, great as that is. The taste of the editor, or of some assistant who uses the scissors, is in a manner forced upon thousands of people, who see little other printed matter than that which he gives them. Suppose his taste runs to murders and abnormal crimes, and to the sensational in literature: what will be the moral effect upon a community of reading this year after year?

If this excess of daily miscellany is deleterious to the public, I doubt if it will be, in the long run, profitable to the newspaper, which has a field broad enough in reporting and commenting upon the movement of the world, without attempting to absorb the whole reading field.

I should like to say a word, if time permitted, upon the form of the journal, and about advertisements. I look to see advertisements shorter, printed with less display, and more numerous. In addition to the use now made of the newspaper by the classes called " advertisers," I expect it to become the handy medium of the entire public, the means of ready communication in regard to all wants and exchanges.

Several years ago, the attention of the publishers of American newspapers was called to the convenient form of certain daily journals in South Germany, which were made up in small pages, the number of which varied from day to day, according to the pressure of news or of advertisements. The suggestion as to form has been adopted by many of our religious, literary, and special weeklies, to the great convenience of the readers, and I doubt not of the publishers also. Nothing is more unwieldly than our big blanket-sheets : they are awkward to handle, inconvenient to read, unhandy to bind and preserve. It is difficult to classify matter in them. In dull seasons they are too large; in times of brisk advertising, and in the sudden access of important news, they are too small. To enlarge them for the occasion, resort is had to a troublesome fly-sheet, or, if they are doubled, there is more space to be filled than is needed. It seems to me that the inevitable remedy is a newspaper of small pages or forms, indefinite in number, that can at any hour be increased or diminished according to necessity, to be folded, stitched, and cut by machinery.

We have thus rapidly run over a prolific field, touching only upon some of the relations of the newspaper to our civilisation, and omitting many of the more important and grave. The truth is that the development of the modern journal has been so sudden and marvellous, that its conductors find themselves in possession of a machine that they scarcely know how to manage or direct. The change in the newspaper caused by the telegraph, the cable, and by a public demand for news created by wars, by discoveries, and by a new outburst of the spirit of doubt and inquiry, is enormous. The public mind is confused about it, and alternately over-estimates and under-estimates the press, failing to see how integral and representative a part it is of modern life.

" The power of the press," as something to be feared or admired, is a favourite theme of dinner-table orators and clergymen. One would think it was some compactly wielded energy, like that of an organised religious order, with a possible danger in it to the public welfare. Discrimination is not made between the power of the printed word — which is limitless — and the influence that a newspaper, as such, exerts. The power of the press is in its facility for making public opinions and events. I should say it is a medium of force rather than force itself. I confess that I am oftener impressed with the powerlessness of the press than otherwise, its slight influence in bringing about any reform, or in inducing the public to do what is for its own good and what it is disinclined to do. Talk about the power of the press, say, in a legislature, when once the members are suspicious that somebody is trying to influence them, and see how the press will retire, with what grace it can, before an invincible and virtuous lobby. The fear of the combination of the press for any improper purpose, or long for any proper purpose, is chimerical. Whomever the newspapers agree with, they do not agree with each other. The public itself never takes so many conflicting views of any topic or event as the ingenious rival journals are certain to discover. It is impossible, in their nature, for them to combine. I should as soon expect agreement among doctors in their empirical profession. And there is scarcely ever a cause, or an opinion, or a man, that does not get somewhere in the press a hearer and a defender.

We will drop the subject with one remark for the benefit of whom it may concern. With all its faults, I believe the moral tone of the American newspaper is higher, as a rule, than that of the community in which it is published.

Certain Diversities of American Life

THIS is a very interesting age. Within the memory of men not yet come to middle life the time of the trotting horse has been reduced from two minutes forty seconds to two minutes eight and a quarter seconds. During the past fifteen years a universal and wholesome pastime of boys has been developed into a great national industry, thoroughly organised and almost altogether relegated to professional hands, no longer the exercise of the million but a spectacle for the million, and a game which rivals the Stock Exchange as a means of winning money on the difference of opinion as to the skill of contending operators.

The newspapers of the country — pretty accurate and sad indicators of the popular taste — devote more daily columns in a week's time to chronicling the news about base-ball than to any other topic that interests the American mind, and the most skilful player, the pitcher, often college bred, whose entire prowess is devoted to not doing what he seems to be doing, and who has become the hero of the American girl as the Olympian wrestler was of the Greek maiden and as the matador is of the Spanish señorita, receives a larger salary for a few hours' exertion each week than any college president is paid for a year's intellectual toil. Such has been the progress in the interest in education during this period that the larger bulk of the news, and that most looked for, printed about the colleges and universities, is that relating to the training, the prospects and achievements of the boat crews and the teams of base-ball and foot-ball, and the victory of any crew or team is a better means of attracting students to its college, a better advertisement, than success in any scholastic contest. A few years ago a tournament was organized in the north between several colleges for competition in oratory and scholarship; it had a couple of contests and then died of inanition and want of public interest.

During the period I am speaking of there has been an enormous advance in technical education, resulting in the establishment of splendid special schools, essential to the development of our national resources; a growth of the popular idea that education should be practical, — that is, such an education as can be immediately applied to earning a living and acquiring wealth speedily, — and an increasing extension of the elective system in colleges, — based almost solely on the notion, having in view, of course, the practical education, that the inclinations of a young man of eighteen are a better guide as to what is best for his mental development and equipment for life than all the experience of his predecessors.

In this period, which you will note is more distinguished by the desire for the accumulation of money than for the general production of wealth, the standard of a fortune has shifted from a fair competence to that of millions of money, so that he is no longer rich who has a hundred thousand dollars, but he only who possesses property valued at many millions, and the men most widely known the country through, most talked about, whose doings and sayings are most chronicled in the journals, whose example is most attractive and stimulating to the minds of youth, are not the scholars, the scientists, the men of letters, not even the orators and statesmen, but those who, by any means, have amassed enormous fortunes. We judge the future of a generation by its ideals.

Regarding education from the point of view of its equipment of a man to make money, and enjoy the luxury which money can command, it must be more and more practical, that is, it must be adapted not even to the higher aim of increasing the general wealth of the world, by increasing production and diminishing waste both of labour and capital, but to the lower aim of getting personal possession of it; so that a striking social feature of the period is that one half — that is hardly an overestimate — one half

of the activity in America of which we speak
with so much enthusiasm, is not directed to
the production of wealth, to increasing its
volume, but to getting the money of other
people away from them. In barbarous ages
this object was accomplished by violence; it
is now attained by skill and adroitness. We
still punish those who gain property by violence; those who get it by smartness and
cleverness, we try to imitate, and sometimes
we reward them with public office.

It appears, therefore, that speed, —the ability to move rapidly from place to place, —
a disproportionate reward of physical over
intellectual science, an intense desire to be
rich, which is strong enough to compel
even education to grind in the mill of the
Philistines, and an inordinate elevation in
public consideration of rich men simply because they are rich, are characteristics of this
little point of time on which we stand. They
are not the only characteristics; in a reasonably optimistic view, the age is distinguished
for unexampled achievements, and for opportunities for the well-being of humanity never

before in all history attainable. But these characteristics are so prominent as to beget the fear that we are losing the sense of the relative value of things in this life.

Few persons come to middle life without some conception of these relative values. It is in the heat and struggle that we fail to appreciate what in the attainment will be most satisfactory to us. After it is over we are apt to see that our possessions do not bring the happiness we expected; or that we have neglected to cultivate the powers and tastes that can make life enjoyable. We come to know, to use a truism, that a person's highest satisfaction depends not upon his exterior acquisitions, but upon what he himself is. There is no escape from this conclusion. The physical satisfactions are limited and fallacious, the intellectual and moral satisfactions are unlimited. In the last analysis, a man has to live with himself, to be his own companion, and in the last resort the question is, what can he get out of himself. In the end, his life is worth just what he has become. And I need not say that the mis-

take commonly made is as to relative values,
— that the things of sense are as important
as the things of the mind. You make that
mistake when you devote your best energies
to your possession of material substance, and
neglect the enlargement, the training, the
enrichment of the mind. You make the
same mistake in a less degree, when you
bend to the popular ignorance and conceit
so far as to direct your college education to
sordid ends. The certain end of yielding to
this so-called practical spirit was expressed
by a member of a northern state legislature
who said, " We don't want colleges, we want
workshops." It was expressed in another
way by a representative of the lower house
in Washington who said, " The average ignorance of the country has a right to be represented here." It is not for me to say whether
it is represented there.

Naturally, I say, we ought by the time of
middle life to come to a conception of what
sort of things are of most value. By analogy, in the continual growth of the Republic,
we ought to have a perception of what we

have accomplished and acquired, and some clear view of our tendencies. We take justifiable pride in the glittering figures of our extension of territory, our numerical growth, in the increase of wealth, and in our rise to the potential position of almost the first nation in the world. A more pertinent inquiry is, what sort of people have we become? What are we intellectually and morally? For after all the man is the thing, the production of the right sort of men and women is all that gives a nation value. When I read of the establishment of a great industrial centre in which twenty thousand people are employed in the increase of the amount of steel in the world, before I decide whether it would be a good thing for the Republic to create another industrial city of the same sort, I want to know what sort of people the twenty thousand are, how they live, what their morals are, what intellectual life they have, what their enjoyment of life is, what they talk about and think about, and what chance they have of getting into any higher life. It does not seem to me a sufficient gain

[84]

in this situation that we are immensely increasing the amount of steel in the world, or that twenty more people are enabled on account of this to indulge in an unexampled, unintellectual luxury. We want more steel, no doubt, but have n't we wit enough to get that and at the same time to increase among the producers of it the number of men and women whose horizons are extended, who are companionable, intelligent beings, adding something to the intellectual and moral force upon which the real progress of the Republic depends?

There is no place where I would choose to speak more plainly of our national situation to-day than in the south, and at the University of the South; in the south, because it is more plainly in a transition state, and at the University of the South, because it is here and in similar institutions that the question of the higher or lower plane of life in the south is to be determined.

To a philosophical observer of the Republic, at the end of the hundred years, I should say that the important facts are not its industrial energy, its wealth, or its population, but the stability of the federal power, and the integrity of the individual States. That is to say, that stress and trial have welded us into an indestructible nation; and not of less consequence is the fact that the life of the Union is in the life of the States. The next most encouraging augury for a great future is the marvellous diversity among the members of this republican body. If nothing would be more speedily fatal to our plan of government than increasing centralisation, nothing would be more hopeless in our development than increasing monotony, the certain end of which is mediocrity.

Speaking as one whose highest pride it is to be a citizen of a great and invincible Republic to those whose minds kindle with a like patriotism, I can say that I am glad there are East and North and South, and West, Middle, Northwest and Southwest, with as many diversities of climate, temperament, habits, idiosyncracies, genius, as these names imply. Thank Heaven we are not all

alike; and so long as we have a common
purpose in the Union, and mutual toleration,
respect, and sympathy, the greater will be
our achievement and the nobler our total
development, if every section is true to the
evolution of its local traits. The superficial
foreign observer finds sameness in our different States, tiresome family likeness in our
cities, hideous monotony in our villages, and
a certain common atmosphere of life, which
increasing facility of communication tends
to increase. This is a view from a railway
train. But as soon as you observe closely,
you find in each city a peculiar physiognomy,
and a peculiar spirit remarkable considering
the freedom of movement and intercourse,
and you find the organised action of each
State *sui generis* to a degree surprising considering the general similarity of our laws
and institutions. In each section differences
of speech, of habits of thought, of temperament prevail. Massachusetts is unlike
Louisiana, Florida unlike Tennessee, Georgia
is unlike California, Pennsylvania is unlike
Minnesota, and so on, and the unlikeness is

not alone or chiefly in physical features. By
the different style of living I can tell when I
cross the line between Connecticut and New
York as certainly as when I cross the line
between Vermont and Canada. The Vir-
ginian expanded in Kentucky is not the
same man he was at home, and the New
England Yankee let loose in the west takes
on proportions that would astonish his grand-
father. Everywhere there is variety in local
sentiment, action, and development. Sit
down in the seats of the State governments
and study the methods of treatment of essentially the common institutions of government, of charity and discipline, and you will
be impressed with the variety of local spirit
and performance in the Union. And this
diversity is so important, this contribution
of diverse elements is so necessary to the
complex strength and prosperity of the
whole, that one must view with alarm all
federal interference and tendency to greater
centralisation.

And not less to be dreaded than monotony from the governmental point of view, is

the obliteration of variety in social life and
in literary development. It is not enough
for a nation to be great and strong, it must
be interesting, and interesting it cannot be
without cultivation of local variety. Better
obtrusive peculiarities than universal sameness. It is out of variety as well as complexity
in American life, and not in homogeneity
and imitation, that we are to expect a civilisation noteworthy in the progress of the
human race.

Let us come a little closer to our subject
in details. For a hundred years the south
was developed on its own lines, with aston-
ishingly little exterior bias. This compara-
tive isolation was due partly to the institution of slavery, partly to devotion to the
production of two or three great staples.
While its commercial connection with the
north was intimate and vital, its literary
relation with the north was slight. With
few exceptions northern authors were not
read in the south, and the literary movement of its neighbours, such as it was, from
1820 to 1860, scarcely affected it. With the

exception of Louisiana, which was absolutely ignorant of American literature and drew its inspiration and assumed its critical point of view almost wholly from the French, the south was English, but mainly English of the time of Walter Scott and George the Third. While Scott was read at the north for his knowledge of human nature, as he always will be read, the chivalric age which moves in his pages was taken more seriously at the south, as if it were of continuing importance in life. In any of its rich private libraries you find yourself in the age of Pope and Dryden, and the classics were pursued in the spirit of Oxford and Cambridge in the time of Johnson. It was little disturbed by the intellectual and ethical agitation of modern England or of modern New England. During this period, while the south excelled in the production of statesmen, orators, trained politicians, great judges, and brilliant lawyers, it produced almost no literature, that is, no indigenous literature, except a few poems and a few humorous character-sketches; its general writing was ornately classic, and its fiction romantic on the lines of the foreign romances.

From this isolation one thing was developed, and another thing might in due time be expected. The thing developed was a social life, in the favoured class, which has an almost unique charm, a power of being agreeable, a sympathetic cordiality, an impulsive warmth, a frankness in the expression of emotion, and that delightful quality of manner which puts the world at ease and makes life pleasant. The southerners are no more sincere than the northerners, but they have less reserve, and in the social traits that charm all who come in contact with them, they have an element of immense value in the variety of American life.

The thing that might have been expected in due time, and when the call came — and it is curious to note that the call and cause of any renaissance are always from the outside — was a literary expression fresh and indigenous. This expectation, in a brief period since the war, has been realised by a remarkable performance and is now stimulated by a remarkable promise. The acclaim with which the southern literature has been received is partly due to its novelty, the new life it exhibited, but more to the recognition in it of a fresh flavour, a literary quality distinctly original and of permanent importance. This production, the first fruits of which are so engaging in quality, cannot grow and broaden into a stable, varied literature without scholarship and hard work, and without a sympathetic local audience. But the momentary concern is that it should develop on its own lines and in its own spirit, and not under the influence of London or Boston or New York. I do not mean by this that it should continue to attract attention by peculiarities of dialect — which is only an incidental, temporary phenomenon, that speedily becomes wearisome, whether "cracker" or negro or Yankee — but by being true to the essential spirit and temperament of southern life.

During this period there was at the north, and especially in the east, great intellectual activity and agitation, and agitation ethical and moral as well as intellectual. There was awakening, investigation, questioning, doubt. There was a great deal of froth thrown to the surface. In the free action of individual thought and expression grew eccentricities of belief and of practice, and a crop of so-called "isms," more or less temporary, unprofitable, and pernicious. Public opinion attained an astonishing degree of freedom, — I never heard of any community that was altogether free of its tyranny. At least extraordinary latitude was permitted in the development of extreme ideas, new, fantastic, radical, or conservative. For instance, slavery was attacked and slavery was defended on the same platform, with almost equal freedom. Indeed, for many years, if there was any exception to the general toleration it was in the social ostracism of those who held and expressed extreme opinions in regard to immediate emancipation, and were stigmatised as abolitionists. There was a general ferment of new ideas, not always fruitful in the direction taken, but hopeful in view of the fact that growth and movement are better than stagnation and decay. You can do something with a ship that has headway; it will drift upon the rocks if it has not. With much foam and froth, sure to attend agitation, there was immense vital energy, intense life.

Out of this stir and agitation came the aggressive, conquering spirit that carried civilisation straight across the continent, that built up cities and States, that developed wealth, and by invention, ingenuity, and energy performed miracles in the way of the subjugation of nature and the assimilation of societies. Out of this free agitation sprang a literary product, great in quantity and to some degree distinguished in quality, groups of historians, poets, novelists, essayists, biographers, scientific writers. A conspicuous agency of the period was the lecture platform, which did something in the spread and popularisation of information, but much more in the stimulation of independent thought and the awakening of the mind to use its own powers.

Along with this and out of this went on

the movement of popular education and of
the high and specialised education. More
remarkable than the achievements of the
common schools has been the development
of the colleges, both in the departments of
the humanities and of science. If I were
writing of education generally, I might have
something to say of the measurable dis-
appointment of the results of the common
schools as at present conducted, both as to
the diffusion of information and as to the
discipline of the mind and the inculcation of
ethical principles; which simply means that
they need improvement. But the higher
education has been transformed, and mainly
by the application of scientific methods, and
of the philosophic spirit, to the study of
history, economics, and the classics. When
we are called to defend the pursuit of metaphysics or the study of the classics, either as
indispensable to the discipline or to the enlargement of the mind, we are not called on
to defend the methods of a generation ago.
The study of Greek is no longer an exercise
in the study of linguistics or the inspection

of specimens of an obsolete literature, but the acquaintance with historic thought, habits, and polity, with a portion of the continuous history of the human mind, which has a vital relation to our own life.

However much or little there may be of permanent value in the vast production of northern literature, judged by continental or even English standards, the time has come when American scholarship in science, in language, in occidental or oriental letters, in philosophic and historical methods, can court comparison with any other. In some branches of research the peers of our scholars must be sought not in England but in Germany. So that in one of the best fruits of a period of intellectual agitation, scholarship, the restless movement has thoroughly vindicated itself.

I have called your attention to this movement in order to say that it was neither accidental nor isolated. It was in the historic line, it was fed and stimulated by all that had gone before, and by all contemporary activity everywhere. New England, for instance, was alert and progressive because it kept its doors and windows open. It was hospitable in its intellectual freedom, both of trial and debate, to new ideas. It was in touch with the universal movement of humanity and of human thought and speculation. You lose some quiet by this attitude, some repose that is pleasant and even desirable perhaps, you entertain many errors, you may try many useless experiments, but you gain life and are in the way of better things. New England, whatever else we may say about it, was in the world. There was no stir of thought, of investigation, of research, of the recasting of old ideas into new forms of life, in Germany, in France, in Italy, in England, anywhere, that did not touch it and to which it did not respond with the sympathy that common humanity has in the universal progress. It kept this touch not only in the evolution and expression of thought and emotion which we call literature (whether original or imitative), but in the application of philosophic methods to education, in the attempted regeneration of society and the amelioration of its conditions by schemes of reform and discipline, relating to the institutions of benevolence and to the control of the vicious and criminal. With all these efforts go along always much false sentimentality and pseudo-philanthropy, but little by little gain is made that could not be made in a state of isolation and stagnation.

In fact there is one historic stream of human thought, aspiration, and progress; it is practically continuous, and with all its diversity of local colour and movement it is a unit. If you are in it, you move; if you are out of it, you are in an eddy. The eddy may have a provincial current, but it is not in the great stream, and when it has gone round and round for a century, it is still an eddy, and will not carry you anywhere in particular. The value of the modern method of teaching and study is that it teaches the solidarity of human history, the continuance of human thought, in literature, government, philosophy, the unity of the divine purpose, and that nothing that has anywhere befallen the human race is alien to us.

I am not undervaluing the part, the important part, played by conservatism, the conservatism that holds on to what has been gained if it is good, that insists on discipline and heed to the plain teaching of experience, that refuses to go into hysterics of enthusiasm over every flighty suggestion, or to follow every leader simply because he proposes something new and strange — I do not mean the conservatism that refuses to try anything simply because it is new, and prefers to energetic life the stagnation that inevitably leads to decay. Isolation from the great historic stream of thought and agitation is stagnation. While this is true, and always has been true in history, it is also true, in regard to the beneficent diversity of American life, which is composed of so many elements and forces, as I have often thought and said, that what has been called the southern conservatism in respect to beliefs and certain social problems, may have a very important part to play in the development of the life of the Republic.

I shall not be misunderstood here, where

the claims of the higher life are insisted on
and the necessity of pure, accurate scholarship is recognised, in saying that this expectation in regard to the south, depends upon
the cultivation and diffusion of the highest
scholarship in all its historic consciousness
and critical precision. This sort of scholarship, of widely apprehending intellectual
activity, keeping step with modern ideas so
far as they are historically grounded, is of the
first importance. Everywhere indeed, in our
industrial age, in a society inclined to mate-
rialism, scholarship, pure and simple scholarship for its own sake, no less in Ohio than in
Tennessee, is the thing to be insisted on.
If I may refer to an institution, which used
to be midway between the north and the
south, and which I may speak of without
suspicion of bias, an institution where the
studies of metaphysics, the philosophy of history, the classics and pure science are as
much insisted on as the study of applied
sciences, the College of New Jersey at
Princeton, the question in regard to a candidate for a professorship or instructorship, is

not whether he was born north or south,
whether he served in one army or another or
in neither, whether he is a Democrat or a
Republican or a Mugwump, what religious
denomination he belongs to, but is he a
scholar and has he a high character? There
is no provincialism in scholarship.

We are not now considering the matter of
the agreeableness of one society or another,
whether life is on the whole pleasanter in
certain conditions at the north or at the south,
whether there is not a charm sometimes in
isolation and even in provincialism. It is a
fair question to ask, what effect upon individual lives and character is produced by an
industrial and commercial spirit, and by one
less restless and more domestic. But the
south is now face to face with certain problems which relate her, inevitably, to the mov-
ing forces of the world. One of these is the
development of her natural resources and
the change and diversity of her industries.
On the industrial side there is pressing need
of institutions of technology, of schools of
applied science, for the diffusion of technical

information and skill in regard to mining and manufacturing, and also to agriculture, so that worn-out lands may be reclaimed and good lands be kept up to the highest point of production. Neither mines, forests, quarries, water-ways, nor textile fabrics can be handled to best advantage without scientific knowledge and skilled labour. The south is everywhere demanding these aids to her industrial development. But just in the proportion that she gets them, and because she has them, will be the need of higher education. The only safety against the influence of a rolling mill is a college, the only safety against the practical and materialising tendency of an industrial school is the increased study of whatever contributes to the higher and non-sordid life of the mind. The south would make a poor exchange for her former condition in any amount of industrial success without a corresponding development of the highest intellectual life.

But, besides the industrial problem, there is the race problem. It is the most serious in the conditions under which it is presented

that ever in all history confronted a free
people. Whichever way you regard it, it
is the nearest insoluble. Under the Constitution it is wisely left to the action of
the individual States. The heavy responsibility is with them. In the nature of things
it is a matter of the deepest concern to the
whole Republic, for the prosperity of every
part is vital to the prosperity of the whole.
In working it out you are entitled, from the
outside, to the most impartial attempt to
understand its real nature, to the utmost
patience with the facts of human nature, to
the most profound and most helpful sympathy. It is monstrous to me that the
situation should be made on either side a
political occasion for private ambition or
for party ends.

I would speak of this subject with the
utmost frankness if I knew what to say. It
is not much of a confession to say that I
do not. The more I study it the less I
know, and those among you who give it
the most anxious thought are the most per-
plexed, the subject has so many conflict-

ing aspects. In the first place there is the evolution of an undeveloped race. Every race has a right to fair play in the world and to make the most of its capacities, and to the help of the more favoured in the attempt. If the suggestion recently made of a wholesale migration to Mexico were carried out, the south would be relieved in many ways, though the labour problem would be a serious one for a long time, but the "elevation" would be lost sight of or relegated to a foreign missionary enterprise; and as for results to the coloured people themselves, there is the example of Hayti. If another suggestion, that of abandoning certain States to this race, were carried out, there is the example of Hayti again, and, besides, an anomaly introduced into the Republic foreign to its traditions, spirit, aspirations, and process of assimilation, alien to the entire historic movement of the Aryan races, and infinitely more dangerous to the idea of the Republic than if solid Ireland were dumped down in the Mississippi valley as an independent State.

On the other hand, there rests upon you the responsibility of maintaining a civilisation — the civilisation of America, not of Hayti or of Guatemala — which we have so hardly won. It is neither to be expected nor desired that you should be ruled by an undeveloped race, ignorant of law, letters, history, politics, political economy. There is no right anywhere in numbers or un-intelligence to rule intelligence. It is a travesty of civilisation. No northern State that I know of would submit to be ruled by an undeveloped race. And human nature is exactly in the south what it is in the north. That is one impregnable fact, to be taken as the basis of all our calculations; the whites of the south will not, cannot, be dominated, as matters now stand, by the coloured race.

But, then, there is the suffrage, the universal, unqualified suffrage. And here is the dilemma. Suffrage once given, cannot be suppressed or denied, perverted by chicane or bribery without incalculable damage to the whole political body. Irregular methods once indulged in for one purpose, and towards one class, so sap the moral sense that they come to be used for all purposes. The danger is ultimately as great to those who suppress or pervert as it is to the suppressed and corrupted. It is the demoralisation of all sound political action and life. I know whereof I speak. In the north, bribery in elections and intimidation are fatal to public morality. The legislature elected by bribery is a bribable body.

I believe that the fathers were right in making government depend upon the consent of the governed. I believe there has been as yet discovered no other basis of government so safe, so stable as popular suffrage, but the fathers never contemplated a suffrage without intelligence. It is a contradiction of terms. A proletariat without any political rights in a republic is no more dangerous than an unintelligent mob which can be used in elections by demagogues. Universal suffrage is not a universal panacea; it may be the best device attainable, but it is certain of abuse without safeguards. One of the absolutely necessary safeguards is an educational qualification. No one ought anywhere to exercise it who cannot read and write, and if I had my way, no one should cast a ballot who had not a fair conception of the effect of it, shown by a higher test of intelligence than the mere fact of ability to scrawl his name and to spell out a line or two in the Constitution. This much the State for its own protection is bound to require, for suffrage is an expediency, not a right belonging to universal humanity regardless of intelligence or of character.

The charge is, with regard to this universal suffrage, that you take the fruits of increased representation produced by it, and then deny it to a portion of the voters whose action was expected to produce a different political result. I cannot but regard it as a blunder in statesmanship to give suffrage without an educational qualification, and to deem it possible to put ignorance over intelligence. You are not responsible for the situation, but you are none the less in an illogical position before the law. Now, would you not gain more in a rectification of your

position than you would lose in other ways,
by making suffrage depend upon an educational qualification? I do not mean gain
party-wise, but in political morals and general
prosperity. Time would certainly be gained
by this, and it is possible in this shifting
world, in the growth of industries and the
flow of populations, that before the question
of supremacy was again upon you, foreign
and industrial immigration would restore
the race balance.

We come now to education. The coloured
race being here, I assume that its education,
with the probabilities this involves of its
elevation, is a duty as well as a necessity.
I speak both of the inherent justice there
is in giving every human being the chance
of bettering his condition and increasing his
happiness that lies in education — unless our
whole theory of modern life is wrong — and
also of the political and social danger there
is in a degraded class numerically strong.
Granted integral membership in a body politic, education is a necessity. I am aware of
the danger of half education, of that smatter-

ing of knowledge which only breeds conceit, adroitness, and a consciousness of physical power, without due responsibility and moral restraint. Education makes a race more powerful both for evil and for good. I see the danger that many apprehend. And the outlook, with any amount of education, would be hopeless, not only as regards the negro and those in neighbourhood relations with him, if education should not bring with it thrift, sense of responsibility as a citizen, and virtue. What the negro race under the most favourable conditions is capable of remains to be shown; history does not help us much to determine thus far. It has always been a long pull for any race to rise out of primitive conditions; but I am sure for its own sake, and for the sake of the republic where it dwells, every thoughtful person must desire the most speedy intellectual and moral development possible of the African race. And I mean as a race.

Some distinguished English writers have suggested, with approval, that the solution of the race problem in this country is fusion,

and I have even heard discouraged southerners accept it as a possibility. The result
of their observation of the amalgamation of
races and colours in Egypt, in Syria, and
Mexico, must be very different from mine.
When races of different colour mingle there
is almost invariably loss of physical stamina,
and the lower moral qualities of each are
developed in the combination. No race
that regards its own future would desire it.
The absorption theory as applied to America
is, it seems to me, chimerical.

But to return to education. It should
always be fitted to the stage of development. It should always mean discipline, the
training of the powers and capacities. The
early pioneers who planted civilisation on
the Watauga, the Holston, the Kentucky,
the Cumberland, had not much broad learning, — they would not have been worse if
they had had more, — but they had courage,
they were trained in self-reliance, virile common sense, and good judgment, they had
inherited the instinct and capacity of self-
government, they were religious, with all

their coarseness they had the fundamental
elements of nobility, the domestic virtues,
and the public spirit needed in the foundation of states. Their education in all the
manly arts and crafts of the backwoodsman,
fitted them very well for the work they had
to do. I should say that the education of
the coloured race in America should be fundamental. I have not much confidence in
an ornamental top-dressing of philosophy,
theology, and classic learning upon the foundation of an unformed and unstable mental
and moral condition. Somehow, character
must be built up, and character depends
upon industry, upon thrift, upon morals,
upon correct ethical perceptions. To have
control of one's powers, to have skill in labour,
so that work in any occupation shall be
intelligent, to have self-respect, which commonly comes from trained capacity, to know
how to live, to have a clean, orderly house, to
be grounded in honesty and the domestic virtues, — these are the essentials of progress.
I suppose that the education to produce
these must be an elemental and practical

one, one that fits for the duties of life and not for some imaginary sphere above them.

To put it in a word, and not denying that there must be schools for teaching the teachers, with the understanding that the teachers should be able to teach what the mass most needs to know—what the race needs for its own good to-day, are industrial and manual training schools, with the varied and practical discipline and arts of life which they impart.

What then? What of the *modus vivendi* of the two races occupying the same soil? As I said before, I do not know. Providence works slowly. Time and patience only solve such enigmas. The impossible is not expected of man, only that he shall do to-day the duty nearest to him. It is easy, you say, for an outsider to preach waiting, patience, forbearance, sympathy, helpfulness. Well, these are the important lessons we get out of history. We struggle, and fume, and fret, and accomplish little in our brief hour, but somehow the world gets on. Fortunately for us, we cannot do to-day the

work of to-morrow. All the gospel in the
world can be boiled down into a single pre-
cept. Do right now. I have observed that
the boy who starts in the morning with a
determination to behave himself till bed-
time, usually gets through the day without
a thrashing.

But of one thing I am sure. In the rush
of industries, in the race problem, it is more
and more incumbent upon such institutions
as the University of the South to maintain
the highest standard of pure scholarship, to
increase the number of men and women
devoted to the intellectual life. Long ago,
in the middle of the seventeenth century,
John Ward of Stratford-on-Avon, clergyman
and physician, wrote in his diary: "The
wealth of a nation depends upon its populousness, and its populousness depends upon
the liberty of conscience that is granted to
it, for this calls in strangers and promotes
trading." Great is the attraction of a benign
climate and of a fruitful soil, but a greater
attraction is an intelligent people, that
values the best things in life, a society

8   [113]

hospitable, companionable, instinct with intellectual life, awake to the great ideas that make life interesting.

As I travel through the south and become acquainted with its magnificent resources and opportunities, and know better and love more the admirable qualities of its people, I cannot but muse in a fond prophecy upon the brilliant part it is to play in the diversified life and the great future of the American Republic. But, north and south, we have a hard fight with materialising tendencies. God bless the University of the South!

The Pilgrim, and the American of To-Day

THIS December evening, the imagination, by a law of contrast, recalls another December night two hundred and seventy years ago. The circle of darkness is drawn about a little group of Pilgrims who have come ashore on a sandy and inhospitable coast. On one side is a vexed and wintry sea, three thousand miles of tossing waves and tempest, beyond which lie the home, the hedgerows and cottages, the church towers, the libraries and universities, the habits and associations of an old civilisation, the strongest and dearest ties that can entwine around a human heart, abandoned now definitely and forever by these wanderers; on the other side a wintry forest of unknown extent, without highways, the lair of wild beasts, impenetrable except by trails known only to the savages, whose sudden appearance and disappearance adds mystery and terror to the impression the imagination has conjured up of the wilderness.

This darkness is symbolic. It stands for a vaster obscurity. This is an encampment on the edge of a continent, the proportions of which are unknown, the form of which is only conjectured. Behind this screen of forest are there hills, great streams, with broad valleys, ranges of mountains perhaps, vast plains, lakes, other wildernesses of illimitable extent? The adventurers on the James hoped they could follow the stream to highlands that looked off upon the South Sea, a new route to India and the Spice Islands. This unknown continent is attacked, it is true, in more than one place. The Dutch are at the mouth of the Hudson; there is a London company on the James; the Spaniards have been long in Florida, and have carried religion and civilisation into the deserts of New Mexico. Nevertheless, the continent, vaster and more varied than was guessed, is practically undiscovered, untrodden. How inadequate to the subjection of any considerable portion of it seems this little band of ill-equipped adventurers, who cannot without peril of life stray a league from the bay where the " Mayflower " lies.

It is not to be supposed that the Pilgrims had an adequate conception of the continent, or of the magnitude of their mission on it, or of the nation to come of which they were laying the foundations. They did the duty that lay nearest to them; and the duty done to-day, perhaps without prescience of its consequences, becomes a permanent stone in the edifice of the future. They sought a home in a fresh wilderness, where they might be undisturbed by superior human authority; they had no doctrinarian notions of equality, nor of the inequality which is the only possible condition of liberty; the idea of toleration was not born in their age; they did not project a republic; they established a theocracy, a church which assumed all the functions of a state, recognising one Supreme Power, whose will in human conduct they were to interpret. Already, however, in the first moment, with a true instinct of self-

government, they drew together in the cabin
of the " Mayflower " in an association to carry
out the divine will in society. But, behold
how speedily their ideas expanded beyond
the Jewish conception, necessarily expanded
with opportunity and the practical self-
dependence of colonies cut off from the aid
of tradition, and brought face to face with
the problems of communities left to themselves. Only a few years later, on the banks
of the Connecticut, Thomas Hooker, the first
American Democrat, proclaimed that "the
foundation of authority is laid in the free
consent of the people," that "the choice of
public magistrates belongs unto the people,
by God's own allowance," that it is the right
of the people not only to choose but to limit
the power of their rulers, and he exhorted,
" as God has given us liberty to *take* it."
There, at that moment, in Hartford, American democracy was born; and in the republican union of the three towns of the
Connecticut colony, Hartford, Windsor, and
Wethersfield, was the germ of the American
federal system, which was adopted into the

federal constitution and known at the time as the " Connecticut Compromise."

It were not worth while for me to come a thousand miles to say this, or to draw over again for the hundredth time the character of the New England Pilgrim, nor to sketch his achievement on this continent. But it is pertinent to recall his spirit, his attitude toward life, and to inquire what he would probably do in the circumstances in which we find ourselves.

It is another December night, before the dawn of a new year. And this night still symbolises the future. You have subdued a continent, and it stands in the daylight radiant with a material splendour of which the Pilgrims never dreamed. Yet a continent as dark, as unknown, exists. It is yourselves, your future, your national life. The other continent was made, you had only to discover it, to uncover it. This you must make yourselves.

We have finished the outline sketch of a magnificent nation. The territory is ample; it includes every variety of climate, in the changing seasons, every variety of physical conformation, every kind of production suited to the wants, almost everything desired in the imagination, of man. It comes nearer than any empire in history to being self-sufficient, physically independent of the rest of the globe. That is to say, if it were shut off from the rest of the world, it has in itself the material for great comfort and civilisation. And it has the elements of motion, of agitation, of life, because the vast territory is filling up with a rapidity unexampled in history. I am not saying that isolated it could attain the highest civilisation, or that if it did touch a high one it could long hold it in a living growth, cut off from the rest of the world. I do not believe it. For no state, however large, is sufficient unto itself. No state is really alive in the highest sense whose receptivity is not equal to its power to contribute to the world with which its destiny is bound up. It is only at its best when it is a part of the vital current of movement, of sympathy, of hope, of enthusiasm of the world at large. There is no doctrine so belittling, so withering to our national life, as that which conceives our destiny to be a life of exclusion of the affairs and interests of the whole globe, hemmed in to the selfish development of our material wealth and strength, surrounded by a Chinese wall built of strata of prejudice on the outside and of ignorance on the inside. Fortunately it is a conception impossible to be realised.

There is something captivating to the imagination in being a citizen of a great nation, one powerful enough to command respect everywhere, and so just as not to excite fear anywhere. This proud feeling of citizenship is a substantial part of a man's enjoyment of life; and there is a certain compensation for hardships, for privations, for self-sacrifice, in the glory of one's own country. It is not a delusion that one can afford to die for it. But what in the last analysis is the object of a government? What is the essential thing, without which even the glory of a nation passes into shame, and the vastness of empire becomes a mockery? I will not say that it is the well-being of every individual, because the term well-being — the *bien être* of the philosophers of the eighteenth century — has mainly a materialistic interpretation, and may be attained by a compromise of the higher life to comfort, and even of patriotism to selfish enjoyment.

That is the best government in which the people, and all the people, get the most out of life; for the object of being in this world is not primarily to build up a government, a monarchy, an aristocracy, a democracy, or a republic, or to make a nation, but to live the best sort of life that can be lived.

We think that our form of government is the one best calculated to attain this end. It is of all others yet tried in this world the one least felt by the people, least felt as an interference in the affairs of private life, in opinion, in conscience, in our freedom to attain position, to make money, to move from place to place, and to follow any career that is open to our ability. In order to maintain this freedom of action, this non-interference, we are bound to resist centralisation of power; for a central power in a republic, grasped and administered by bosses, is no more tolerable than central power in a despotism, grasped and administered by a hereditary aristocrat. Let us not be deceived by names. Government by the consent of the people is the best government, but it is not government by the people when it is in the hands of political bosses, who juggle with the theory of majority rule. What republics have most to fear is the rule of the boss, who is a tyrant without responsibility. He makes the nominations, he dickers and trades for the elections, and at the end he divides the spoils. The operation is more uncertain than a horse race, which is not decided by the speed of the horses, but by the state of the wagers and the manipulation of the jockeys. We strike directly at his power for mischief when we organise the entire civil service of the nation and of the States on capacity, integrity, experience, and not on political power.

And if we look further, considering the danger of concentration of power in irresponsible hands, we see a new cause for alarm in undue federal mastery and interference. This we can only resist by the constant assertion of the rights, the power, the dignity of the individual State, all that it has not surrendered in the fundamental constitution of the Republic. This means the full weight of the State, as a State, as a political unit, in the election of President; and the full weight of the State, as a State, as a political unit, without regard to its population, in the senate of the United States. The senate, as it stands, as it was meant to be in the Constitution, is the strongest safeguard which the fundamental law established against centralisation, against the tyranny of mere majorities, against the destruction of liberty, in such a diversity of climates and conditions as we have in our vast continent. It is not a mere check upon hasty legislation; like some second chambers in Europe, it is the representative of powers whose preservation in their dignity is essential to the preservation of the form of our government itself.

We pursue the same distribution of power and responsibility when we pass to the States.

The federal government is not to interfere in what the State can do and ought to do for itself; the State is not to meddle with what the county can best do for itself; nor the county in the affairs best administered by the town and the municipality. And so we come to the individual citizen. He cannot delegate his responsibility. The government even of the smallest community must be, at least is, run by parties and by party machinery. But if he wants good government, he must pay as careful attention to the machinery, — call it caucus, primary, convention, town-meeting, — as he does to the machinery of his own business. If he hands it over to bosses, who make politics a trade for their own livelihood, he will find himself in the condition of stockholders of a bank whose directors are mere dummies, when some day the cashier packs the assets and goes on a foreign journey for his health. When the citizen simply does his duty in the place where he stands, the boss will be eliminated, in the nation, in the State, in the town, and we shall have, what by courtesy we say we have now, a government by the people. Then all the way down from the capital to the city ward, we shall have vital popular government, free action, discussion, agitation, life. What an anomaly it is, that a free people, reputed shrewd and intelligent, should intrust their most vital interests, the making of their laws, the laying of their taxes, the spending of their money, even their education and the management of their public institutions into the keeping of political bosses, whom they would not trust to manage the least of their business affairs, nor to arbitrate on what is called a trial of speed at an agricultural fair.

But a good government, the best government is only an opportunity. However vast the country may become in wealth and population, it cannot rise in quality above the average of the majority of its citizens; and its goodness will be tested in history by its value to the average man, not by its bigness, not by its power, but by its adaptability to the people governed, so as to develop the best that is in them. It is incidental and imperative that the country should be an agreeable one to live in; but it must be more than that, it must be favourable to the growth of the higher life. The Puritan community of Massachusetts Bay, whose spirit we may happily contrast with that of the Pilgrims whose anniversary we celebrate, must have been as disagreeable to live in as any that history records; not only were the physical conditions of life hard, but its inquisitorial intolerance overmatched that which it escaped in England. It was a theocratic despotism, untempered by recreation or amusement, and repressive not only of freedom of expression but of freedom of thought. But it had an unconquerable will, a mighty sense of duty, a faith in God, which not only established its grip upon the continent but carried its influence from one ocean to the other. It did not conquer by its bigotry, by its intolerance, its cruel persecuting spirit, but by its higher mental and spiritual stamina. These lower and baser qualities of the age of the Puritans leave a stain upon a great achievement; it took

[127]

Massachusetts almost two centuries to cast them off and come into a wholesome freedom, but the vital energy and the recognition of the essential verities in human life carried all the institutions of the Puritans that were life-giving over the continent.

Here in the west you are near the centre of a vast empire, you feel its mighty pulse, the throb and heart-beat of its immense and growing strength. Some of you have seen this great civilisation actually grow on the vacant prairies, in the unoccupied wilderness, on the sandy shores of the inland seas. You have seen the trails of the Indian and the deer replaced by highways of steel, and upon the spots where the first immigrants corralled their wagons, and the voyagers dragged their canoes upon the reedy shore, you have seen arise great cities, centres of industry, of commerce, of art, attaining in a generation the proportions and the world-wide fame of cities that were already famous before the discovery of America.

Naturally the country is proud of this achievement. Naturally we magnify our material prosperity. But in this age of science and invention this development may be said to be inevitable, and besides it is the necessary out-let of the energy of a free people. There must be growth of cities, extension of railways, improvement of agriculture, development of manufactures, amassing of wealth, concentration of capital, beautifying of homes, splendid public buildings, private palaces, luxury, display. Without reservoirs of wealth there would be no great universities, schools of science, museums, galleries of art, libraries, solid institutions of charity, and perhaps not the wide diffusion of culture which is the avowed aim of modern civilisation.

But this in its kind is an old story. It is an experiment that has been repeated over and over. History is the record of the rise of splendid civilisations, many of which have flowered into the most glorious products of learning and of art, and have left monuments of the proudest material achievements. Except in the rapidity with which steam and electricity have enabled us to move to our

9

object, and in the discoveries of science which enable us to relieve suffering and prolong human life, there is nothing new in our experiment. We are pursuing substantially the old ends of material success and display. And the ends are not different because we have more people in a nation, or bigger cities with taller buildings, or more miles of railway, or grow more corn and cotton, or make more ploughs and threshing-machines, or have a greater variety of products than any nation ever had before. I fancy that a pleased visitor from another planet the other day at Chicago, who was shown an assembly much larger than ever before met under one roof, might have been interested to know that it was also the wisest, the most cultivated, the most weighty in character of any assembly ever gathered under one roof.

Our experiment on this continent was intended to be something more than the creation of a nation on the old pattern, that should become big and strong, and rich and luxurious, divided into classes of the very

wealthy and the very poor, of the enlightened and the illiterate. It was intended
to be a nation in which the welfare of the
people is the supreme object, and whatever
its show among nations it fails if it does
not become this. This welfare is an individual matter, and it means many things.
It includes in the first place physical comfort for every person willing and deserving
to be physically comfortable, decent lodging,
good food, sufficient clothing. It means, in
the second place, that this shall be an agreeable country to live in, by reason of its
impartial laws, social amenities, and a fair
chance to enjoy the gifts of nature and
Providence. And it means, again, the opportunity to develop talents, aptitudes for
cultivation and enjoyment, in short, freedom
to make the most possible out of our lives.
This is what Jefferson meant by the " pursuit of happiness; " it was what the constitution meant by the " general welfare," and
what it tried to secure in States, safe-guarded
enough to secure independence in the play
of local ambition and home rule, and in a

federal republic strong enough to protect the whole from foreign interference. We are in no vain chase of an inequality which would eliminate all individual initiative, and check all progress, by ignoring differences of capacity and strength, and rating muscles equal to brains. But we are in pursuit of equal laws, and a fairer chance of leading happy lives than humanity in general ever had yet. And this fairer chance would not, for instance, permit any man to become a millionaire by so manipulating railways that the subscribing towns and private stock-holders should lose their investments; nor would it assume that any Gentile or Jew has the right to grow rich by the chance of compelling poor women to make shirts for six cents apiece. The public opinion which sustains these deeds is as un-American, and as guilty as their doers. While abuses like these exist, tolerated by the majority that not only make public opinion, but make the laws, this is not a government for the people, any more than a government of bosses is a government by the people.

The Pilgrims of Plymouth could see no way of shaping their lives in accordance with the higher law except by separating themselves from the world. We have their problem, how to make the most of our lives, but the conditions have changed. Ours is an age of scientific aggression, fierce competition, and the widest toleration. The horizon of humanity is enlarged. To live the life now is to be no more isolated or separate, but to throw ourselves into the great movement of thought, and feeling, and achievement. Therefore we are altruists in charity, missionaries of humanity, patriots at home. Therefore we have a justifiable pride in the growth, the wealth, the power of the nation, the state, the city. But the stream cannot rise above its source. The nation is what the majority of its citizens are. It is to be judged by the condition of its humblest members. We shall gain nothing over other experiments in government, although we have money enough to buy peace from the rest of the world, or arms enough to conquer it, although we rear upon our material prosperity a structure of scientific achievement, of art, of literature unparalleled, if the common people are not sharers in this great prosperity, and are not fuller of hope and of the enjoyment of life than common people ever were before.

And we are all common people when it comes to that. Whatever the greatness of the nation, whatever the accumulation of wealth, the worth of the world to us is exactly the worth of our individual lives. The magnificent opportunity in this Republic is that we may make the most possible out of our lives, and it will continue only as we adhere to the original conception of the Republic. Politics without virtue, money-making without conscience, may result in great splendour, but as such an experiment is not new, its end can be predicted. An agreeable home for a vast, and a free, and a happy people is quite another thing. It expects thrift, it expects prosperity, but its foundations are in the moral and spiritual life.

Therefore I say that we are still to make

the continent we have discovered and occupied, and that the scope and quality of our national life are still to be determined. If they are determined not by the narrow tenets of the Pilgrims, but by their high sense of duty, and of the value of the human soul, it will be a nation that will call the world up to a higher plane of action than it ever attained before, and it will bring in a new era of humanity. If they are determined by the vulgar successes of a mere material civilisation, it is an experiment not worth making. It would have been better to have left the Indians in possession, to see if they could not have evolved out of their barbarism some new line of action.

The Pilgrims were poor, and they built their huts on a shore which gave such niggardly returns for labour that the utmost thrift was required to secure the necessaries of life. Out of this struggle with nature and savage life was no doubt evolved the hardihood, the endurance, that builds states and wins the favours of fortune. But poverty is not commonly a nurse of virtue, long continued, it is a degeneration. It is almost as difficult for the very poor man to be virtuous as for the very rich man; and very good and very rich at the same time, says Socrates, a man cannot be. It is a great people that can withstand great prosperity. The condition of comfort without extremes is that which makes a happy life. I know a village of old-fashioned houses and broad elm-shaded streets in New England, indeed more than one, where no one is inordinately rich, and no one is very poor, where paupers are so scarce that it is difficult to find beneficiaries for the small traditionary contribution for the church poor; where the homes are centres of intelligence, of interest in books, in the news of the world, in the church, in the school, in politics; whence go young men and women to the colleges, teachers to the illiterate parts of the land, missionaries to the city slums. Multiply such villages all over the country, and we have one of the chief requisites for an ideal republic.

This has been the longing of humanity.

Poets have sung of it; prophets have had visions of it; statesmen have striven for it; patriots have died for it. There must be somewhere, sometime, a fruitage of so much suffering, so much sacrifice, a land of equal laws and equal opportunities, a government of all the people for the benefit of all the people; where the conditions of living will be so adjusted that every one can make the most out of his life, neither waste it in hopeless slavery nor in selfish tyranny, where poverty and crime will not be hereditary generation after generation, where great fortunes will not be for vulgar ostentation, but for the service of humanity and the glory of the state, where the privileges of freemen will be so valued that no one will be mean enough to sell his vote nor corrupt enough to attempt to buy a vote, where the truth will at last be recognised, that the society is not prosperous when half its members are lucky, and half are miserable, and that that nation can only be truly great that takes its orders from the Great Teacher of Humanity.

[137]

And, lo! at last here is a great continent, virgin, fertile, a land of sun and shower and bloom, discovered, organised into a great nation, with a government flexible in a distributed home rule, stiff as steel in a central power, already rich, already powerful. It is a land of promise. The materials are all here. Will you repeat the old experiment of a material success and a moral and spiritual failure? Or will you make it what humanity has passionately longed for? Only good individual lives can do that.

Nathan Hale

IN a Memorial Day address at New Haven in 1881, the Hon. Richard D. Hubbard suggested the erection of a statue to Nathan Hale in the State Capitol. With the exception of the monument in Coventry no memorial of the young hero existed. The suggestion was acted on by the Hon. E. S. Cleveland, who introduced a resolution in the House of Representatives in the session of 1883, appropriating money for the purpose. The propriety of this was urged before a committee of the Legislature by Governor Hubbard, in a speech of characteristic grace and eloquence, seconded by the Hon. Henry C. Robinson and the Hon. Stephen W. Kellogg. The Legislature appropriated the sum of five thousand dollars for a statue in bronze, and a committee was appointed to procure it. They opened a public competition, and, after considerable delay, during which the commission was

changed by death and by absence, — indeed
four successive governors, Hubbard, Waller,
Harrison and Lounsbury have served on it,
— the work was awarded to Karl Gerhardt,
a young sculptor who began his career in
this city. It was finished in clay, and accepted in October, 1886, put in plaster, and
immediately sent to the foundery of Melzar
Masman in Chicopee, Massachusetts.

To-day in all its artistic perfection and
beauty it stands here to be revealed to the
public gaze. It is proper that the citizens
of Connecticut should know how much of
this result they owe to the intelligent zeal
of Mr. Cleveland, the mover of the resolution in the Legislature, who in the commission, and before he became a member of it,
has spared neither time nor effort to procure
a memorial worthy of the hero and of the
State. And I am sure that I speak the unan-
imous sentiment of the commission in the
regret that the originator of this statue could
not have seen the consummation of his idea,
and could not have crowned it with the one
thing lacking on this occasion, the silver

words of eloquence we always heard from his lips, that compact, nervous speech, the perfect union of strength and grace; for who so fitly as the lamented Hubbard could have portrayed the moral heroism of the Martyr-Spy?

This is not a portrait statue. There is no likeness of Nathan Hale extant. The only known miniature of his face, in the possession of the lady to whom he was betrothed at the time of his death, disappeared many years ago. The artist was obliged, therefore, to create an ideal figure, aided by a few fragmentary descriptions of Hale's personal appearance. His object has been to represent an American youth of the period, an American patriot and scholar, whose manly beauty and grace tradition loves to recall, to represent in face and in bearing the moral elevation of character that made him conspicuous among his fellows, and to show forth, if possible, the deed that made him immortal. For it is the deed and the memorable last words we think of when we think of Hale. I know

that by one of the canons of art it is held
that sculpture should rarely fix a momentary action; but if this can be pardoned
in the Laocoön, where suffering could not
otherwise be depicted to excite the sympathy
of the spectator, surely it can be justified in
this case, where, as one may say, the immortality of the subject rests upon a single act,
upon a phrase, upon the attitude of the
moment. For all the man's life, all his
character, flowered and blossomed into immortal beauty in this one supreme moment
of self-sacrifice, triumph, defiance. The ladder of the gallows-tree on which the de-
serted boy stood, amidst the enemies of his
country, when he uttered those last words
which all human annals do not parallel in
simple patriotism, — the ladder I am sure
ran up to heaven, and if angels were not seen
ascending and descending it in that gray
morning, there stood the embodiment of
American courage, unconquerable, American faith, invincible, American love of
country, unquenchable, a new democratic
manhood in the world, visible there for

all men to take note of, crowned already
with the halo of victory in the Revolu-
tionary dawn. Oh, my Lord Howe! it
seemed a trifling incident to you and to
your bloodhound, Provost Marshal Cunningham, but those winged last words were worth
ten thousand men to the drooping patriot
army. Oh, your Majesty, King George the
Third! here was a spirit, could you but have
known it, that would cost you an empire,
here was an ignominious death that would
grow in the estimation of mankind, increasing in nobility above the fading pageantry
of kings.

On the 21st of April, 1775, a messenger,
riding express from Boston to New York
with the tidings of Lexington and Concord,
reached New London. The news created
intense excitement. A public meeting was
called in the court-house at twilight, and
among the speakers who exhorted the people
to take up arms at once, was one, a youth
not yet twenty years of age, who said, " Let
us march immediately, and never lay down
our arms until we have obtained our inde-

pendence,"—one of the first, perhaps the first, of the public declarations of the purpose of independence. It was Nathan Hale, already a person of some note in the colony, of a family then not unknown and destined in various ways to distinction in the Republic. A kinsman of the same name lost his life in the Louisburg fight. He had been for a year the preceptor of the Union Grammar School at New London. The morning after the meeting he was enrolled as a volunteer, and soon marched away with his company to Cambridge.

Nathan Hale, descended from Robert Hale who settled in Charlestown in 1632, a scion of the Hales of Kent, England, was born in Coventry, Connecticut, on the 6th of June, 1755, the sixth child of Richard Hale and his wife Elizabeth Strong, persons of strong intellect and the highest moral character, and Puritans of the strictest observances. Brought up in this atmosphere, in which duty and moral rectitude were the unquestioned obligations in life, he came to manhood with a character that enabled him to

face death or obloquy without flinching, when
duty called, so that his behaviour at the last
was not an excitement of the moment, but
the result of ancestry, training, and principle.
Feeble physically in infancy, he developed
into a robust boy, strong in mind and body,
a lively, sweet-tempered, beautiful youth, and
into a young manhood endowed with every
admirable quality. In feats of strength and
agility he recalls the traditions of Washington; he early showed a remarkable avidity
for knowledge, which was so sought that he
became before he was of age one of the best
educated young men of his time in the colonies. He was not only a classical scholar,
with the limitations of those days; but, what
was then rare, he made scientific attainments
which greatly impressed those capable of
judging, and he had a taste for art and a
remarkable talent as an artist. His father
intended him for the ministry. He received
his preparatory education from Dr. Joseph
Huntington, a classical scholar and the pastor
of the church in Coventry, entered Yale College at the age of sixteen, and graduated with

high honours in a class of sixty, in September, 1773. At the time of his graduation his personal appearance was notable. Dr. Enos Monroe of New Haven, who knew him well in the last year at Yale, said of him : —

"He was almost six feet in height, perfectly proportioned, and in figure and deportment he was the most manly man I have ever met. His chest was broad; his muscles were firm; his face wore a most benign expression; his complexion was roseate; his eyes were light blue and beamed with intelligence ; his hair was soft and light brown in colour, and his speech was rather low, sweet, and musical. His personal beauty and grace of manner were most charming. Why, all the girls in New Haven fell in love with him," said Dr. Munro, "and wept tears of real sorrow when they heard of his sad fate. In dress he was always neat; he was quick to lend a hand to a being in distress, brute or human; was overflowing with good humour, and was the idol of all his acquaintances."

Dr. Jared Sparks, who knew several of Hale's intimate friends, writes of him : —

"Possessing genius, taste, and order, he became distinguished as a scholar; and endowed in an eminent degree with those graces and gifts of Nature which add a charm to youthful excellence, he gained universal esteem and confidence. To high moral worth and irreproachable habits were joined gentleness of manner, an ingenuous disposition, and vigour of understanding. No young man of his years put forth a fairer promise of future usefulness and celebrity; the fortunes of none were fostered more sincerely by the generous good wishes of his superiors."

It was remembered at Yale that he was a brilliant debater as well as scholar. At his graduation he engaged in a debate on the question, "Whether the education of daughters be not, without any just reason, more neglected than that of the sons." "In this debate," wrote James Hillhouse, one of his classmates, "he was the champion of the daughters, and most ably advocated their cause. You may be sure that he received the plaudits of the ladies present."

Hale seems to have had an irresistible charm for everybody. He was a favourite in society; he had the manners and the qualities that made him a leader among men and gained him the admiration of women. He was always intelligently busy, and had the Yankee ingenuity, — he "could do anything but spin," he used to say to the girls of Coventry, laughing over the spinning wheel. There is a universal testimony to his alert intelligence, vivacity, manliness, sincerity, and winningness.

It is probable that while still an undergraduate at Yale, he was engaged to Alice Adams, who was born in Canterbury, a young lady distinguished then as she was afterwards for great beauty and intelligence. After Hale's death she married Mr. Eleazer Ripley, and was left a widow at the age of eighteen, with one child, who survived its father only one year. She married, the second time, William Lawrence, Esq., of Hartford, and died in this city, greatly respected and admired, in 1845, aged eighty-eight. It is a touching note of the hold the memory of her young hero had upon her admiration that her last words, murmured as life was ebbing, were, "Write to Nathan."

Hale's short career in the American army need not detain us. After his flying visit as a volunteer to Cambridge, he returned to New London, joined a company with the rank of lieutenant, participated in the siege of Boston, was commissioned a captain in the Nineteenth Connecticut Regiment in January, 1776, performed the duties of a soldier with vigilance, bravery, and patience, and was noted for the discipline of his company. In the last dispiriting days of 1775, when the terms of his men had expired, he offered to give them his month's pay if they would remain a month longer. He accompanied the army to New York, and shared its fortunes in that discouraging spring and summer. Shortly after his arrival Captain Hale distinguished himself by the brilliant exploit of cutting out a British sloop, laden with provisions, from under the guns of the man-of-war " Asia," sixty-four, lying in the East River, and bringing her triumphantly into slip. During the summer he suffered a severe illness.

The condition of the American army and cause on the 1st of September, 1776, after the retreat from Long Island, was critical. The army was demoralised, clamouring in vain for pay, and deserting by companies

and regiments; one third of the men were
without tents, one fourth of them were on
the sick list. On the 7th, Washington called
a council of war, and anxiously inquired what
should be done. On the 12th, it was determined to abandon the city, and take possession of Harlem Heights. The British army,
twenty-five thousand strong, admirably
equipped, and supported by a powerful naval
force, threatened to envelop our poor force,
and finish the war in a stroke. Washington
was unable to penetrate the designs of the
British commander, or to obtain any trusty
information of the intentions or the movements of the British army. Information was
imperatively necessary to save us from destruction, and it could only be obtained by
one skilled in military and scientific knowledge and a good draughtsman, a man of
quick eye, cool head, tact, sagacity, and
courage, and one whose judgment and fidelity
could be trusted. Washington applied to
Lieutenant-Colonel Knowlton, who sum-
moned a conference of officers in the name
of the commander-in-chief, and laid the mat-

ter before them. No one was willing to undertake the dangerous and ignominious mission. Knowlton was in despair, and late in the conference was repeating the necessity, when a young officer, pale from recent illness, entered the room and said, " I will undertake it." It was Captain Nathan Hale. Everybody was astonished. His friends besought him not to attempt it. In vain. Hale was under no illusion. He silenced all remonstrances by saying that he thought he owed his country the accomplishment of an object so important and so much desired by the commander-in-chief, and he knew no way to obtain the information except by going into the enemy's camp in disguise. " I wish to be useful," he said; "and every kind of service necessary for the public good becomes honourable by being necessary. If the exigencies of my country demand a peculiar service, its claims to the performance of that service are imperious."

The tale is well known. Hale crossed over from Norwalk to Huntington Cove on Long Island. In the disguise of a schoolmaster, he penetrated the British lines and the city, made accurate drawings of the fortifications, and memoranda in Latin of all that he observed, which he concealed between the soles of his shoes, and returned to the point on the shore where he had first landed. He expected to be met by a boat and to cross the Sound to Norwalk the next morning. The next morning he was captured, no doubt by Tory treachery, and taken to Howe's headquarters, the mansion of James Beekman, situated at (the present) 50th Street and First Avenue. That was on the 21st of September. Without trial and upon the evidence found on his person, Howe condemned him to be hanged as a spy early next morning. Indeed Hale made no attempt at defence. He frankly owned his mission, and expressed regret that he could not serve his country better. His open, manly bearing and high spirit commanded the respect of his captors. Mercy he did not expect, and pity was not shown him. The British were irritated by a conflagration which had that morning laid almost a third of the city in ashes, and which they attributed to incendiary efforts to deprive them of agreeable winter quarters. Hale was at first locked up in the Beekman greenhouse. Whether he remained there all night is not known, and the place of his execution has been disputed; but the best evidence seems to be that it took place on the farm of Colonel Rutger, on the west side, in the orchard in the vicinity of the present East Broadway and Market Street, and that he was hanged to the limb of an apple-tree.

It was a lovely Sunday morning, before the break of day, that he was marched to the place of execution, September 22nd. While awaiting the necessary preparations, a courteous young officer permitted him to sit in his tent. He asked for the presence of a chaplain; the request was refused. He asked for a Bible; it was denied. But at the solicitation of the young officer he was furnished with writing materials, and wrote briefly to his mother, his sister, and his betrothed. When the infamous Cunningham, to whom Howe had delivered him, read what was written, he was furious at the noble and dauntless spirit shown, and with foul oaths tore the letters into shreds, saying afterwards "that the rebels should never know that they had a man who could die with such firmness." As Hale stood upon the fatal ladder, Cunningham taunted him, and tauntingly demanded his "last dying speech and confession." The hero did not heed the words of the brute, but, looking calmly upon the spectators, said in a clear voice, "I only regret that I have but one life to lose for my country." And the ladder was snatched from under him.

My friends, we are not honouring to-day a lad who appears for a moment in a heroic light, but one of the most worthy of the citizens of Connecticut, who has by his lofty character long honoured her, wherever patriotism is not a mere name, and where Christian manhood is respected. We have had many heroes, many youths of promise, and men of note, whose names are our only great and enduring riches; but no one of them all better illustrated, short as was his career, the

virtues we desire for all our sons. We have
long delayed this tribute to his character and
his deeds, but in spite of our neglect his fame
has grown year by year, as war and politics
have taught us what is really admirable in a
human being, and we are now sure that we
are not erecting a monument to an ephemeral
reputation.

It is fit that it should stand here, one of
the chief distinctions of our splendid Capitol,
here in the political centre of the State, here
in the city where first in all the world was
proclaimed and put into a political charter
the fundamental idea of democracy, that
"government rests upon the consent of the
people," here in the city where by the action
of these self-existing towns was formed the
model, the town and the commonwealth, the
bi-cameral legislature, of our constitutional
federal union.

If the soul of Nathan Hale, immortal in
youth in the air of heaven, can behold to-day
this scene, as doubtless it can, in the midst
of a State whose prosperity the young colo-
nist could not have imagined in his wildest

dreams for his country, he must feel anew the truth that there is nothing too sacred for a man to give for his native land.

Governor Lounsbury, the labour of the commission is finished. On their behalf I present this work of art to the State of Connecticut.

Let the statue speak for itself.

Some Causes of the Prevailing Discontent

THE Declaration of Independence opens with the statement of a great and fruitful political truth. But if it had said:—"We hold these truths to be self-evident: that all men are created *un*-equal; that they are endowed by their Creator with certain inalienable rights; that among these are life, liberty and the pursuit of happiness," it would also have stated the truth; and if it had added, "All men are born in society with certain duties which cannot be disregarded without danger to the social state," it would have laid down a necessary corollary to the first declaration. No doubt those who signed the document understood that the second clause limited the first, and that men are created equal only in respect to certain rights. But the first part of the clause has been taken alone as the statement of a self-evident truth, and the attempt to make this unlimited phrase a reality has caused a great deal of misery. In connection with the neglect of the idea that the recognition of certain duties is as important as the recognition of rights in the political and social state — that is, in connection with the doctrine of *laissez faire* — this popular notion of equality is one of the most disastrous forces in modern society.

Doubtless men might have been created equal to each other in every respect, with the same mental capacity, the same physical ability, with like inheritances of good or bad qualities, and born into exactly similar conditions, and not dependent on each other. But men never were so created and born, so far as we have any record of them, and by analogy we have no reason to suppose that they ever will be. Inequality is the most striking fact in life. Absolute equality might be better, but so far as we can see, the law of the universe is infinite diversity in unity; and variety in condition is the essential of what we call progress — it is, in fact, life. The great doctrine of the Christian era — the brotherhood of man and the duty of the strong to the weak — is in sharp contrast with this doctrinarian notion of equality. The Christian religion never proposed to remove the inequalities of life or its suffering, but by the incoming of charity and contentment and a high mind to give individual men a power to be superior to their conditions.

It cannot, however, be denied that the spirit of Christianity has ameliorated the condition of civilised peoples, co-operating in this with beneficent inventions. Never were the mass of the people so well fed, so well clad, so well housed, as to-day in the United States. Their ordinary daily comforts and privileges were the luxuries of a former age, often indeed unknown and unattainable to the most fortunate and privileged classes. Nowhere else is it or was it so easy for a man to change his condition, to satisfy his wants, nowhere else has he or had he such advantages of education, such facilities of travel, such an opportunity to find an environment to suit himself. As a rule the mass of mankind have been tied to the spot where they were born. A mighty change has taken place in regard to liberty, freedom of personal action, the possibility of coming into contact with varied life and an enlarged participation in the bounties of nature and the inventions of genius. The whole world is in motion, and at liberty to be so. Everywhere that civilisation has gone there is an immense improvement in material conditions during the last one hundred years.

And yet men were never so discontented, nor did they ever find so many ways of expressing their discontent. In view of the general amelioration of the conditions of life this seems unreasonable and illogical, but it may seem less so when we reflect that human nature is unchanged, and that which has to be satisfied in this world is the mind. And there are some exceptions to this general material prosperity, in its result to the working classes. Manufacturing England is an exception. There is nothing so pitiful, so hopeless in the record of man, not in the Middle Ages, not in rural France just before the Revolution, as the physical and mental condition of the operators in the great manufacturing cities and in the vast reeking slums of London. The political economists have made England the world's great workshop, on the theory that wealth is the greatest good in life, and that with the golden streams flowing into England from a tributary world, wages would rise, food be cheap, employment constant. The horrible result to humanity is one of the exceptions to the general uplift of the race, not paralleled as yet by anything in this country, but to be taken note of as a possible outcome of any material civilisation, and fit to set us thinking whether we have not got on a wrong track. Mr. Froude, fresh from a sight of the misery of industrial England, and borne straight on toward Australia over a vast ocean, through calm and storm, by a great steamer, — horses of fire yoked to a sea-chariot, — exclaims : " What, after all, have these wonderful achievements done to elevate human nature?

Human nature remains as it was. Science grows, but morality is stationary, and art is vulgarised. Not here lie the 'things necessary to salvation,' not the things which can give to human life grace, or beauty, or dignity."

In the United States, with its open opportunities, abundant land, where the condition of the labouring class is better actually and in possibility than it ever was in history, and where there is little poverty except that which is inevitably the accompaniment of human weakness and crime, the prevailing discontent seems groundless. But of course an agitation so wide-spread, so much in earnest, so capable of evoking sacrifice, even to the verge of starvation and the risk of life, must have some reason in human nature. Even an illusion — and men are as ready to die for an illusion as for a reality — cannot exist without a cause.

Now, content does not depend so much upon a man's actual as his relative condition. Often it is not so much what I need, as what others have that disturbs me. I should be content to walk from Boston to New York, and be a fortnight on the way, if everybody else was obliged to walk who made that journey. It becomes a hardship when my neighbour is whisked over the route in six hours and I have to walk. It would still be a hardship if he attained the ability to go in an hour, when I was only able to accomplish the distance in six hours. While there has been a tremendous uplift all along the line of material conditions, and the labouring man who is sober and industrious has comforts and privileges in his daily life which the rich man who was sober and industrious did not enjoy a hundred years ago, the relative position of the rich man and the poor man has not greatly changed. It is true, especially in the United States, that the poor have become rich and the rich poor, but inequality of condition is about as marked as it was before the invention of labour-saving machinery, and though working men are better off in many ways, the accumulation of vast fortunes, acquired often in brutal disregard of humanity, marks the contrast of conditions perhaps more emphatically than it ever appeared before. That this inequality should continue in an era of universal education, universal suffrage, universal locomotion, universal emancipation from nearly all tradition, is a surprise, and a perfectly comprehensible cause of discontent. It is axiomatic that all men are created equal. But, somehow, the problem does not work out in the desired actual equality of conditions. Perhaps it can be forced to the right conclusion by violence.

It ought to be said, as to the United States, that a very considerable part of the discontent is imported, it is not native, nor based on any actual state of things existing here. Agitation has become a business. A great many men and some women, to whom work of any sort is distasteful, live by it. Some of them are refugees from military or political despotism, some are refugees from justice, some from the lowest conditions of industrial slavery. When they come here, they assume that the hardships they have come away to escape exist here, and they

begin agitating against them. Their business is to so mix the real wrongs of our
social life with imaginary hardships, and to
heighten the whole with illusory and often
debasing theories, that discontent will be
engendered.   For it is by means of that only
that they live.   It requires usually a great
deal of labour, of organisation, of oratory to
work up this discontent so that it is profitable.   The solid working men of America
who know the value of industry and thrift,
and have confidence in the relief to be
obtained from all relievable wrongs by legitimate political or other sedate action, have no
time to give to the leadership of agitations
which require them to quit work, and destroy industries, and attack the social order
upon which they depend.   The whole case,
you may remember, was embodied thousands
of years ago in a parable, which Jotham,
standing on the top of Mount Gerizim, spoke
to the men of Shechem:

"The trees went forth on a time to anoint
a king over them; and they said unto the
olive-tree, 'Reign thou over us.'

" But the olive-tree said unto them, 'Should I leave my fatness wherewith by me they honour God and man, and go to be promoted over the trees?'

" And the trees said to the fig-tree, ' Come thou and reign over us.'

" But the fig-tree said unto them, ' Should I forsake my sweetness and my good fruit, and go to be promoted over the trees?'

" Then said the trees unto the vine, ' Come thou and reign over us.'

" And the vine said unto them, 'Should I leave my wine, which cheereth God and man, and go to be promoted over the trees?'

" Then said the trees unto the bramble, 'Come thou and reign over us.'

" And the bramble said to the trees, ' If in truth ye anoint me king over you, then come and put your trust in my shadow ; and if not, let fire come out of the bramble, and devour the cedars of Lebanon.' "

In our day a conflagration of the cedars of Lebanon has been the only result of the kingship of the bramble.

In the opinion of many, our universal education is one of the chief causes of the discontent. This might be true and not be an argument against education, for a certain amount of discontent is essential to self-development; and if, as we believe, the development of the best powers of every human being is a good in itself, education ought not to be held responsible for the evils attending a transitional period. Yet we cannot ignore the danger, in the present stage, of an education that is necessarily superficial, that engenders conceit of knowledge and power, rather than real knowledge and power, and that breeds in two-thirds of those who have it a distaste for useful labour. We believe in education; but there must be something wrong in an education that sets so many people at odds with the facts of life, and, above all, does not furnish them with any protection against the wildest illusions. There is something wanting in the education that only half educates people.

Whether there is the relation of cause and effect between the two I do not pretend to say, but universal and superficial education in this country has been accompanied with the most extraordinary delusions and the evolution of the wildest theories. It is only necessary to refer, by way of illustration, to the greenback illusion, and to the whole group of spiritualistic disturbances and psychological epidemics. It sometimes seems as if half the American people were losing the power to apply logical processes to the ordinary affairs of life.

In studying the discontent in this country which takes the form of a labour movement, one is at first struck by its illogical aspects. So far as it is an organised attempt to better the condition of men by association of interests it is consistent. But it seems strange that the doctrine of individualism should so speedily have an outcome in a personal slavery, only better in the sense that it is voluntary, than that which it protested against. The revolt from authority, the assertion of the right of private judgment, has been pushed forward into a socialism which destroys individual liberty of action, or to a state of anarchy in which the weak would have no protection. I do not imagine that the leaders who preach socialism, who live by agitation and not by labour, really desire to overturn the social order and bring chaos. If social chaos came, their occupation would be gone, for if all men were reduced to a level, they would be compelled to scratch about with the rest for a living. They live by agitation, and they are confident that government will be strong enough to hold things together, so that they can continue agitation.

The strange thing is that their followers who live by labour and expect to live by it, and believe in the doctrine of individualism, and love liberty of action, should be willing to surrender their discretion to an arbitrary committee, and should expect that liberty of action would be preserved if all property were handed over to the state, which should undertake to regulate every man's time, occupation, wages, and so on. The central committee or authority, or whatever it might be called, would be an extraordinary des-

potism, tempered only by the idea that it
could be overturned every twenty-four hours.
But what security would there be for any
calculations in life in a state of things in expectation of a revolution any moment?
Compared with the freedom of action in
such a government as ours, any form of
communism is an iniquitous and meddle-
some despotism.   In a less degree an association to which a man surrenders the right
to say when, where, and for how much he
shall work, is a despotism, and when it goes
further and attempts to put a pressure on all
men outside of the association, so that they
are free neither to work nor to hire the
workmen they choose, it is an extraordinary
tyranny.   It almost puts in the shade Mexi-
can or Russian personal government.   A demand is made upon a railway company that
it shall discharge a certain workman because
and only because he is not a member of the
union.   The company refuses.   Then a distant committee orders a strike on that road,
which throws business far and wide into confusion, and is the cause of heavy loss to tens

of thousands who have no interest in any association of capital or labour, many of whom are ruined by this violence. Some of the results of this surrender of personal liberty are as illegal as illogical.

The boycott is a conspiracy to injure another person, and as such indictable at common law. A strike, if a conspiracy only to raise wages or to reduce hours of labour, may not be indictable, if its object cannot be shown to be the injury of another, though that may be incidentally its effect. But in its incidents, such as violence, intimidation, and in some cases injury to the public welfare, it often becomes an indictable offence. The law of conspiracy is the most ill-defined branch of jurisprudence, but it is safe to say of the boycott and the strike that they both introduce an insupportable element of tyranny, of dictation, of interference, into private life. If they could be maintained, society would be at the mercy of an irresponsible and even secret tribunal.

The strike is illogical. Take the recent experience in this country. We have had a long season of depression, in which many earned very little and labour sought employment in vain. In the latter part of winter the prospect brightened, business revived, orders for goods poured in to all the factories in the country, and everybody believed that we were on the eve of a very prosperous season. This was the time taken to order strikes, and they were enforced in perhaps a majority of cases against the wishes of those who obeyed the order, and who complained of no immediate grievance. What men chiefly wanted was the opportunity to work. The result has been to throw us all back into the condition of stagnation and depression. Many people are ruined, an immense amount of capital which ventured into enterprises is lost, but of course the greatest sufferers are the working men themselves.

The methods of violence suggested by the communists and anarchists are not remedial. Real difficulties exist, but these do not reach them. The fact is that people in any relations incur mutual obligations, and the

world cannot go on without a recognition of
duties as well as rights. We all agree that
every man has a right to work for whom he
pleases, and to quit the work if it does not
or the wages do not suit him. On the other
hand, a man has a right to hire whom he
pleases, pay such wages as he thinks he can
afford, and discharge men who do not suit
him. But when men come together in the
relation of employer and employed, other
considerations arise. A man has capital
which, instead of loaning at interest or lock-
ing up in real estate or bonds, he puts into
a factory. In other words, he unlocks it for
the benefit partly of men who want wages.
He has the expectation of making money, of
making more than he could by lending his
money. Perhaps he will be disappointed,
for a common experience is the loss of capital thus invested. He hires workmen at
certain wages. On the strength of this
arrangement, he accepts orders and makes
contracts for the delivery of goods. He
may make money one year and lose the
next. It is better for the workman that he

should prosper, for the fund of capital accumulated is that upon which they depend to give them wages in a dull time. But some day when he is in a corner with orders, and his rivals are competing for the market, and labour is scarce, his men strike on him.

Conversely, take the workman settled down to work in the mill, at the best wages attainable at the time. He has a house and family. He has given pledges to society. His employer has incurred certain duties in regard to him by the very nature of their relations. Suppose the workman and his family cannot live in any comfort on the wages he receives. The employer is morally bound to increase the wages if he can. But if, instead of sympathising with the situation of his workman, he forms a combination with all the mills of his sort, and reduces wages merely to increase his gains, he is guilty of an act as worthy of indictment as the strike. I do not see why a conspiracy against labour is not as illegal as a conspiracy against capital. The truth is, the possession of power by men or associations makes them selfish and generally cruel. Few employers consider anything but the arithmetic of supply and demand in fixing wages, and working men who have the power, tend to act as selfishly as the male printers used to act in striking in an establishment which dared to give employment to women type-setters. It is of course sentimental to say it, but I do not expect we shall ever get on with less friction than we have now, until men recognise their duties as well as their rights in their relations with each other.

In running over some of the reasons for the present discontent, and the often illogical expression of it, I am far from saying anything against legitimate associations for securing justice and fair play. Disassociated labour has generally been powerless against accumulated capital. Of course, organised labour-getting power will use its power (as power is always used) unjustly and tyrannically. It will make mistakes, it will often injure itself while inflicting general damage. But with all its injustice, with all its surrender of personal liberty, it seeks to call the

attention of the world to certain hideous
wrongs, to which the world is likely to
continue selfishly indifferent unless rudely
shaken out of its sense of security. Some
of the objects proposed by these associations
are chimerical, but the agitation will doubtless go on until another element is introduced into work and wages than mere supply
and demand. I believe that sometime it
will be impossible that a woman shall be
forced to make shirts at six cents a piece,
with the gaunt figures of starvation or a life
of shame waiting at the door. I talked recently with the driver of a street-car in a
large city. He received a dollar and sixty
cents a day. He went on to his platform at
eight in the morning, and left it at twelve
at night, sixteen hours of continuous labour
every day in the week. He had no rest for
meals, only snatched what he could eat as he
drove along, or at intervals of five or eight
minutes at the end of routes. He had no
Sunday, no holiday in the year. Between
twelve o'clock at night and eight the next
morning, he must wash and clean his car.

Thus his hours of sleep were abridged. He was obliged to keep an eye on the passengers to see that they put their fares in the box, to be always responsible for them, that they got on and off without accident, to watch that the rules were enforced, and that collisions and common street dangers were avoided. This mental and physical strain for sixteen consecutive hours, with scant sleep, so demoralised him that he was obliged once in two or three months to hire a substitute and go away to sleep. This is treating a human being with less consideration than the horses receive. He is powerless against the great corporation; if he complains, his place is instantly filled; the public does not care.

Now what I want to say about this case, and that of the woman who makes a shirt for six cents (and these are only types of disregard of human souls and bodies that we are all familiar with), is that if society remains indifferent it must expect that organisations will attempt to right them, and the like wrongs, by ways violent and destructive of the innocent and guilty alike. It is human nature, it is the lesson of history, that real wrongs, unredressed, grow into preposterous demands. Men are much like nature in action; a little disturbance of atmospheric equilibrium becomes a cyclone, a slight break in the levee a crevasse with immense destructive power.

In considering the growth of discontent, and of a natural disregard of duties between employers and employed, it is to be noted that while wages in nearly all trades are high, the service rendered deteriorates, less conscience is put into the work, less care to give a fair day's work for a fair day's wages, and that pride in good work is vanishing. This may be in the nature of retaliation for the indifference to humanity taught by a certain school of political economists, but it is, nevertheless, one of the most alarming features of these times. How to cultivate the sympathy of the employers with the employed as men, and how to interest the employed in their work beyond the mere wages they receive, is the double problem.

As the intention of this paper was not to

suggest remedies, but only to review some of
the causes of discontent, I will only say, as to
this double problem, that I see no remedy so
long as the popular notion prevails that the
greatest good of life is to make money
rapidly, and while it is denied that all men
who contribute to prosperity ought to share
equitably in it. The employed must recognise the necessity of an accumulated fund of
capital, and on the other hand the employer
must be as anxious to have about him a contented, prosperous community, as to heap up
money beyond any reasonable use for it.
The demand seems to be reasonable that the
employer in a prosperous year ought to share
with the workmen the profits beyond a limit
that capital, risk, enterprise, and superior
skill can legitimately claim; and that on the
other hand the workmen should stand by the
employer in hard times.

Discontent, then, arises from absurd notions of equality, from natural conditions of
inequality, from false notions of education,
and from the very patent fact, in this age,
that men have been educated into wants

much more rapidly than social conditions have been adjusted, or perhaps ever can be adjusted, to satisfy those wants.   Beyond all the actual hardship and suffering, there is an immense mental discontent which has to be reckoned with.

This leads me to what I chiefly wanted to say in this paper, to the cause of discontent which seems to me altogether the most serious, altogether the most difficult to deal with.   We may arrive at some conception of it, if we consider what it is that the well-to-do, the prosperous, the rich, the educated and cultivated portions of society, most value just now.

If, to take an illustration which is sufficiently remote to give us the necessary perspective, if the political economists, the manufacturers, the traders and aristocracy of England had had chiefly in mind the development of the labouring people of England into a fine type of men and women, full of health and physical vigour, with minds capable of expansion and enjoyment, the creation of decent, happy, and contented homes, would they have reared the industrial fabric we now see there? If they had not put the accumulation of wealth above the good of individual humanity, would they have turned England into a grimy and smoky workshop, commanding the markets of the world by cheap labour, condemning the mass of the people to unrelieved toil and the most squalid and degraded conditions of life in towns, while the land is more and more set apart for the parks and pleasure grounds of the rich? The policy pursued has made England the richest of countries, a land of the highest refinement and luxury for the upper classes, and of the most misery for the great mass of common people. On this point we have but to read the testimony of English writers themselves. It is not necessary to suppose that the political economists were inhuman. They no doubt believed that if England attained this commanding position, the accumulated wealth would raise all classes into better conditions. Their mistake is that of all peoples who have made money their first object. Looked at merely on the material side, you would think that what a philanthropic statesman would desire, who wished a vigorous, prosperous nation, would be a strong and virile population, thrifty and industrious, and not mere slaves of mines and mills, degenerating in their children, year by year, physically and morally. But apparently they have gone upon the theory that it is money, not man, that makes a state.

In the United States, under totally different conditions, and under an economic theory that, whatever its defects on paper, has nevertheless insisted more upon the worth of the individual man, we have had, all the same, a distinctly material development. When foreign critics have commented upon this, upon our superficiality, our commonplaceness, what they are pleased to call the weary level of our mediocrity, upon the raging unrest and race for fortune, and upon the tremendous pace of American life, we have said that this is incident to a new country and the necessity of controlling physical conditions, and of fitting our heterogeneous population to their environment. It is hardly to be expected, we have said, until we have the leisure that comes from easy circumstances and accumulated wealth, that we should show the graces of the highest civilisation, in intellectual pursuits. Much of this criticism is ignorant, and to say the best of it, ungracious, considering what we have done in the way of substantial appliances for education, in the field of science, in vast charities, and missionary enterprises, and what we have to show in the diffused refinements of life.

We are already wealthy; we have greater resources and higher credit than any other nation; we have more wealth than any save one; we have vast accumulations of fortune, in private hands and in enormous corporations. There exists already, what could not be said to exist a quarter of a century ago, a class who have leisure. Now what is the object in life of this great, growing class that has money and leisure, what does it chiefly care for? In your experience of society, what is it that it pursues and desires? Is it things of the mind or things of the senses? What is it that interests women, men of for-

tune, club-men, merchants, and professional
men whose incomes give them leisure to follow their inclinations, the young men who
have inherited money? Is it political duties,
the affairs of state, economic problems, some
adjustment of our relations that shall lighten
and relieve the wrongs and misery everywhere apparent; is the interest in intellectual pursuits and art (except in a dilettante
way dictated for a season by fashion) in
books, in the wide range of mental pleasures
which make men superior to the accidents of
fortune? Or is the interest of this class, for
the most part, with some noble exceptions,
rather in things grossly material, in what is
called pleasure? To come to somewhat vulgar details, is not the growing desire for
dress, for sumptuous houses, for showy equi-
pages, for epicurean entertainments, for display, either refined or ostentatious, rivalry in
profusion and expense, new methods for kill-
ing time, for every imaginable luxury, which
is enjoyed partly because it pleases the senses,
and partly because it satisfies an ignoble
craving for class distinction?

I am not referring to these things as a moralist at all, but simply in their relation to popular discontent.   The astonishing growth of luxury and the habit of sensual indulgence are seen everywhere in this country, but are most striking in the city of New York, since the fashion and wealth of the whole country meet there for display and indulgence, — New York, which rivals London and outdoes Paris in sumptuousness.   There congregates more than elsewhere idlers, men and women of leisure who have nothing to do except to observe or to act in the spectacle of Vanity Fair.   Aside from the display of luxury in the shops, in the streets, in private houses, one is impressed by the number of idle young men and women of fashion.

It is impossible that a working man who stands upon a metropolitan street corner and observes this Bacchanalian revel and prodigality of expense, should not be embittered by a sense of the inequality of the conditions of life.   But this is not the most mischievous effect of the spectacle.   It is the example of what these people care for.   With all their

wealth and opportunities, it seems to him that
these select people have no higher object than
the pleasures of the senses, and he is taught
daily by reiterated example that this is the end
and aim of life. When he sees the value
the intelligent and the well-to-do set upon
material things, and their small regard for
intellectual things and the pleasures of the
mind, why should he not most passionately
desire those things which his more fortunate
neighbours put foremost?   It is not the sight
of a Peter Cooper and his wealth that discon-
tents him, nor the intellectual pursuits of the
scholar who uses the leisure his fortune gives
him for the higher pleasures of the mind.
But when society daily dins upon his senses
the lesson that not manhood and high thinking and a contented spirit are the most
desirable things, whether one is rich or poor,
is he to be blamed for having a wrong notion
of what will or should satisfy him? What
the well-to-do, the prosperous, are seen to
value most in life will be the things most
desired by the less fortunate in accumulation.
It is not so much the accumulation of money

that is mischievous in this country, for the most stupid can see that fortunes are constantly shifting hands, but it is the use that is made of the leisure and opportunity that money brings.

Another observation, which makes men discontented with very slow accumulation, is that, apparently, in the public estimation it does not make much difference whether a man acquires wealth justly or unjustly. If he only secures enough, he is a power, he has social position, he grasps the high honours and places in the state. The fact is that the toleration of men who secure wealth by well known dishonest and sharp practices is a chief cause of the demoralisation of the public conscience.

However the lines social and political may be drawn, we have to keep in mind that nothing in one class can be foreign to any other, and that practically one philosophy underlies all the movements of an age. If our philosophy is material, resulting in selfish ethics, all our energies will have a materialistic tendency. It is not to be wondered at, therefore, that, in a time when making money is the chief object, if it is not reckoned the chief good, our education should all tend to what is called practical, that is, to that which can be immediately serviceable in some profitable occupation of life, to the neglect of those studies which are only of use in training the intellect and cultivating, and broadening the higher intelligence. To this purely material and utilitarian idea of life, the higher colleges and universities everywhere are urged to conform themselves. Thus is the utilitarian spirit eating away the foundations of a higher intellectual life, applying to everything a material measure. In proportion as scholars yield to it, they are lowering the standard of what is most to be desired in human life, acting in perfect concert with that spirit which exalts money making as the chief good, which makes science itself the slave of the avaricious and greedy, and fills all the world with discontented and ignoble longing. We do not need to be told that if we neglect pure science for the pursuit of applied science only, applied science will speedily be degraded and un-fruitful; and it is just as true that if we pursue knowledge only for the sake of gain, and not for its own sake, knowledge will lose the power it has of satisfying the higher needs of the human soul. If we are seen to put only a money value on the higher education, why should not the working man, who regards it only as a distinction of class or privilege, estimate it by what he can see of its practical results in making men richer, or bringing him more pleasure of the senses?

The world is ruled by ideas, by abstract thought. Society, literature, art, politics, in any given age are what the prevailing system of philosophy makes them. We recognise this clearly in studying any past period. We see, for instance, how all the currents of human life changed upon the adoption of the inductive method; no science, no literature, no art, practical or fine, no person, inquiring scholar, day labourer, trader, sailor, fine lady or humblest housekeeper, escaped the influence. Even though the prevailing ethics may teach that every man's highest duty is to himself, we cannot escape community of sympathy and destiny in this cold-blooded philosophy.

No social or political movement stands by itself. If we inquire, we shall find one preponderating cause underlying every movement of the age. If the utilitarian spirit is abroad, it accounts for the devotion to the production of wealth, and to the consequent separation of classes and the discontent, and it accounts also for the demand that all education shall be immediately useful. I was talking the other day with a lady who was doubting what sort of an education to give her daughter, a young girl of exceedingly fine mental capacity. If she pursued a classical course, she would, at the age of twenty-one, know very little of the sciences. And I said, why not make her an intellectual woman? At twenty-one, with a trained mind, all knowledges are at one's feet.

If anything can correct the evils of devotion to money, it seems to me that it is the production of intellectual men and women, who will find other satisfactions in life than those of the senses. And when labour sees what it is that is really most to be valued, its discontent will be of a nobler kind.

The Education of the Negro

A T the close of the war for the Union about five millions of negroes were added to the citizenship of the United States. By the census of 1890 this number had become over seven and a half millions. I use the word negro, because the descriptive term black or coloured is not determinative. There are many varieties of negroes among the African tribes, but all of them agree in certain physiological if not psychological characteristics, which separate them from all other races of mankind; whereas there are many races, black or coloured, like the Abyssinian, which have no other negro traits.

It is also a matter of observation that the negro traits persist in recognisable manifestations, to the extent of occasional reversions, whatever may be the mixture of a white race. In a certain degree this per-

sistence is true of all races not come from
an historic common stock.

In the political reconstruction the negro
was given the ballot without any requirements of education or property. This was
partly a measure of party balance of power;
and partly from a concern that the negro
would not be secure in his rights as a citizen
without it, and also upon the theory that the
ballot is an educating influence.

This sudden transition and shifting of
power was resented at the south, resisted at
first, and finally it has generally been evaded.
This was due to a variety of reasons or prejudices, not all of them creditable to a generous desire for the universal elevation of
mankind, but one of them the historian will
judge adequate to produce the result. Indeed, it might have been foreseen from
the beginning. This reconstruction measure
was an attempt to put the superior part of
the community under the control of the
inferior, — these parts separated by all
the prejudices of race, and by traditions of
mastership on the one side and of servi-

tude on the other. I venture to say that it was an experiment that would have failed in any community in the United States, whether it was presented as a piece of philanthropy or of punishment.

A necessary sequence to the enfranchisement of the negro was his education. However limited our idea of a proper common education may be, it is a fundamental requisite in our form of government that every voter should be able to read and write. A recognition of this truth led to the establishment in the south of public schools for the whites and blacks, — in short of a public school system. We are not to question the sincerity and generousness of this movement, however it may have halted and lost enthusiasm in many localities.

This opportunity of education (found also in private schools) was hailed by the negroes, certainly, with enthusiasm. It cannot be doubted that at the close of the war there was a general desire among the freedmen to be instructed in the rudiments of knowledge at least. Many parents, especially women, made great sacrifices to obtain for their children this advantage which had been denied to themselves. Many youths, both boys and girls, entered into it with a genuine thirst for knowledge which it was pathetic to see.

But it may be questioned, from developments that speedily followed, whether the mass of negroes did not really desire this advantage as a sign of freedom, rather than from a wish for knowledge, and covet it because it had formerly been the privilege of their masters, and marked a broad distinction between the races. It was natural that this should be so, when they had been excluded from this privilege by pains and penalties, when in some States it was one of the gravest offences to teach a negro to read and write. This prohibition was accounted for by the peculiar sort of property that slavery created, which would become insecure if intelligent, for the alphabet is a terrible disturber of all false relations in society.

But the effort at education went further than the common school and the primary essential instruction. It introduced the higher education. Colleges — usually called universities — for negroes were established in many southern States, created and stimulated by the generosity of northern men and societies, and often aided by the liberality of the States where they existed. The curriculum in these was that in colleges generally, — the classics, the higher mathematics, science, philosophy, the modern languages, and in some instances a certain technical instruction, which was being tried in some northern colleges. The emphasis, however, was laid on liberal culture. This higher education was offered to the mass that still lacked the rudiments of intellectual training, in the belief that education — the education of the moment, the education of superimposed information, can realise the theory of universal equality.

This experiment has now been in operation long enough to enable us to judge something of its results and its promises for the future. These results are of a nature to lead us seriously to inquire whether our effort was founded upon an adequate knowledge of the negro, of his present development, of the requirements for his personal welfare and evolution in the scale of civilisation, and for his training in useful and honourable citizenship. I am speaking of the majority, the mass to be considered in any general scheme, and not of the exceptional individuals — exceptions that will rapidly increase as the mass is lifted — who are capable of taking advantage to the utmost of all means of cultivation, and who must always be provided with all the opportunities needed.

Millions of dollars have been invested in the higher education of the negro, while this primary education has been, taking the whole mass, wholly inadequate to his needs. This has been upon the supposition that the higher would compel the rise of the lower with the undeveloped negro race as it does with the more highly developed white race. An examination of the soundness of this expectation will not lead us far astray from our subject.

The evolution of a race, distinguishing it

from the formation of a nation, is a slow process. We recognise a race by certain peculiar traits, and by characteristics which slowly change. They are acquired little by little in an evolution which, historically, it is often difficult to trace. They are due to the environment, to the discipline of life, and to what is technically called education. These work together to make what is called character, race character, and it is this which is transmitted from generation to generation. Acquirements are not hereditary, like habits and peculiarities, physical or mental. A man does not transmit to his descendants his learning, though he may transmit the aptitude for it. This is illustrated in factories where skilled labour is handed down and fixed in the same families, that is, where the same kind of labour is continued from one generation to another. The child, put to work, has not the knowledge of the parent, but a special aptitude in his skill and dexterity. Both body and mind have acquired certain transmissible traits. The same thing is seen on a larger scale in a whole nation, like the Japanese, who have been trained into what seems an art instinct.

It is this character, quality, habit, the result of a slow educational process, which distinguishes one race from another. It is this that the race transmits, and not the more or less accidental education of a decade or an era. The Brahmins carry this idea into the next life, and say that the departing spirit carries with him nothing except this individual character, no acquirements or information or extraneous culture. It was perhaps in the same spirit that the sad preacher in Ecclesiastes said, there is no " knowledge nor wisdom in the grave, whither thou goest."

It is by this character that we classify civilised and even semi-civilised races; by this slowly developed fibre, this slow accumulation of inherent quality in the evolution of the human being from lower to higher, that continues to exist notwithstanding the powerful influence of governments and religions. We are understood when we speak of the French, the Italian, the Pole, the Spanish, the English, the German, the Arab race, the Japanese, and so on. It is what a foreign writer calls, not inaptly, a collective race soul. As it is slow in evolution, it is persistent in enduring.

Further, we recognise it as a stage of progress, historically necessary in the development of man into a civilised adaptation to his situation in this world. It is a process that cannot be much hurried, and a result that cannot be leaped to out of barbarism by any superimposition of knowledge or even quickly by any change of environment. We may be right in our modern notion that education has a magical virtue that can work any kind of transformation; but we are certainly not right in supposing that it can do this instantly, or that it can work this effect upon a barbarous race in the same period of time that it can upon one more developed, one that has acquired at least a race consciousness.

Before going further, and in order to avoid misunderstanding, it is proper to say that I have the firmest belief in the ultimate development of all mankind into a higher plane than it occupies now. I should otherwise be in despair. This faith will never desist in the effort to bring about the end desired. But, if we work with Providence, we must work in the reasonable ways of Providence, and add to our faith, patience.

It seems to be the rule in all history that the elevation of a lower race is effected only by contact with one higher in civilisation. Both reform and progress come from exterior influences. This is axiomatic, and applies to the fields of government, religion, ethics, art, and letters.

We have been taught to regard Africa as a dark, stolid continent, unawakened, unvisited by the agencies and influences that have transformed the world from age to age. Yet it was in northern and northeastern Africa that within historic periods three of the most powerful and brilliant civilisations were developed, — the Egyptian, the Carthaginian, the Saracenic. That these civilisations had more than a surface contact with the interior, we know. To take the most

ancient of them, and that which longest endured, the Egyptian, the Pharaohs carried
their conquests and their power deep into
Africa. In the story of their invasions and
occupancy of the interior, told in pictures on
temple walls, we find the negro figuring as
captive and slave. This contact may not
have been a fruitful one for the elevation of
the negro, but it proves that for ages he was
in one way or another in contact with a superior civilisation. In later days we find
little trace of it in the home of the negro,
but in Egypt the negro has left his impress
in the mixed blood of the Nile valley.

The most striking example of the contact
of the negro with a higher civilisation is in
the powerful mediæval empire of Songhay,
established in the heart of the negro country. The vast strip of Africa lying north of
the equator and south of the twentieth parallel and west of the upper Nile, was then, as
it is now, the territory of tribes distinctly described as Negro. The river Niger running
northward from below Jenne to near Timbuctoo, and then turning west and south to

the Gulf of Guinea, flows through one of the richest valleys in the world. In richness it is comparable to that of the Nile, and like that of the Nile its fertility depends upon the water of the central stream. Here arose in early times the powerful empire of Songhay, which disintegrated and fell into tribal confusion about the middle of the seventeenth century. For a long time the seat of its power was the city of Jenne, in later days it was Timbuctoo.

This is not the place to enlarge upon this extraordinary piece of history. The best account of the empire of Songhay is to be found in the pages of Barth, the German traveller, who had access to what seemed to him a credible Arab history. Considerable light is thrown upon it by a recent volume on Timbuctoo by M. Dubois, a French traveller. M. Dubois finds reason to believe that the founders of the Songhese empire came from Yemen, and sought refuge from Moslem fanaticism in Central Africa some hundred and fifty years after the Hejira. The origin of the empire is obscure, but the development was not indigenous. It seems probable that the settlers, following traders, penetrated to the Niger valley from the valley of the Nile as early as the third or fourth century of our era. An evidence of this early influence, which strengthened from century to century, Dubois finds in the architecture of Jenne and Timbuctoo. It is not Roman or Saracenic or Gothic, it is distinctly Pharaonic. But whatever the origin of the Songhay empire, it became in time Mohammedan, and so continued to the end. Mohammedanism seems, however, to have been imposed. Powerful as the empire was, it was never free from tribal insurrection and internal troubles. The highest mark of negro capacity developed in this history is, according to the record examined by Barth, that one of the emperors was a negro.

From all that can be gathered in the records, the mass of the negroes, which constituted the body of this empire, remained pagan, did not become, except in outward conformity, Mohammedan and did not take the Moslem civilisation as it was developed elsewhere, and that the disintegration of the empire left the negro races practically where they were before in point of development. This fact, if it is not overturned by further search, is open to the explanation that the Moslem civilisation is not fitted to the development of the African negro.

Contact, such as it has been, with higher civilisations, has not in all these ages which have witnessed the wonderful rise and development of other races, much affected or changed the negro. He is much as he would be if he had been left to himself. And left to himself, even in such a favourable environment as America, he is slow to change. In Africa there has been no progress in organisation, government, art. No negro tribe has ever invented a written language. In his exhaustive work on the History of Mankind, Professor Frederick Ratzel, having studied thoroughly the negro belt of Africa, says, " of writing properly so called, neither do the modern negroes show any trace, nor have traces of older writing been found in negro countries."

From this outline review we come back to the situation in the United States, where a great mass of negroes — possibly over nine millions of many shades of colours — is for the first time brought into contact with Christian civilisation. This mass is here to make or mar our national life, and the problem of its destiny has to be met with our own. What can we do, what ought we to do, for his own good and for our peace and national welfare?

In the first place, it is impossible to escape the profound impression that we have made a mistake in our estimate of his evolution as a race, in attempting to apply to him the same treatment for the development of character that we would apply to a race more highly organised. Has he developed the race consciousness, the race soul, as I said before, a collective soul, which so strongly marks other races more or less civilised according to our standards? Do we find in him, as a mass (individuals always excepted), that slow deposit of training and education called " character," any firm basis of order, initiative of action, the capacity of going alone, any sure foundation of morality? It has been said that a race may attain a good degree of standing in the world without the refinement of culture, but never without virtue, either in the Roman or the modern meaning of that word.

The African, now the American negro, has come in the United States into a more favourable position for development than he has ever before had offered. He has come to it through hardship, and his severe apprenticeship is not ended. It is possible that the historians centuries hence, looking back over the rough road that all races have travelled in their evolution, may reckon slavery and the forced transportation to the new world, a necessary step in the training of the negro. We do not know. The ways of Providence are not measurable by our foot rules. We see that slavery was unjust, uneconomic, and the worst training for citizenship in such a government as ours. It stifled a number of germs that might have produced a better development, such as individuality, responsibility, and thrift, — germs absolutely necessary to the well-being of a race. It laid no foundation of morality, but in place of morality saw cultivated a superstitious, emotional, hysterical religion. It is true that it taught a savage race subordination and obedience. Nor did it stifle certain inherent temperamental virtues, faithfulness, often highly developed, and frequently cheerfulness and philosophic contentment in a situation that would have broken the spirit of a more sensitive race. In short, under all the disadvantages of slavery the race showed certain fine traits, qualities of humour, and good humour, and capacity for devotion, which were abundantly testified to by southerners during the progress of the Civil War. It has, as a race, traits wholly distinct from those of the whites, which are not only interesting but might be a valuable contribution to a cosmopolitan civilisation ; gifts also, such as the love of music, and temperamental gayety, mixed with a note of sadness, as in the Hungarians.

But slavery brought about one result, and

that the most difficult in the development
of a race from savagery, and especially a
tropical race, a race that has always been
idle in the luxuriance of a nature that sup-
plied its physical needs with little labour.
It taught the negro to work, it transformed
him, by compulsion it is true, into an industrial being and held him in the habit of
industry for several generations. Perhaps
only force could do this, for it was a radical
transformation. I am glad to see that this
result of slavery is recognised by Mr. Booker
Washington, the ablest and most clear-
sighted leader the negro race has ever
had.

But something more was done under this
pressure, something more than creation of
a habit of physical exertion to productive
ends. Skill was developed. Skilled labour,
which needs brains, was carried to a high
degree of performance. On almost all the
southern plantations, and in the cities also,
negro mechanics were bred, excellent black-
smiths, good carpenters, and house-builders
capable of executing plans of high archi-

tectural merit. Everywhere were negroes skilled in trades, and competent in various mechanical industries.

The opportunity and the disposition to labour make the basis of all our civilisation. The negro was taught to work, to be an agriculturist, a mechanic, a material producer of something useful. He was taught this fundamental thing. Our higher education, applied to him in his present development, operates in exactly the opposite direction.

This is a serious assertion. Its truth or falsehood cannot be established by statistics, but it is an opinion gradually formed by experience, and the observation of men competent to judge, who have studied the problem close at hand. Among the witnesses to the failure of the result expected from the establishment of colleges and universities for the negro, are heard, from time to time, and more frequently as time goes on, practical men from the north, railway men, manufacturers, who have initiated business enterprises at the south. Their testimony coincides with that of careful students of the economic and social conditions.

There was reason to assume, from our theory and experience of the higher education in its effect upon white races, that the result would be different from what it is. When the negro colleges first opened, there was a glow of enthusiasm, an eagerness of study, a facility of acquirement, and a good order that promised everything for the future. It seemed as if the light then kindled would not only continue to burn, but would penetrate all the dark and stolid communities. It was my fortune to see many of these institutions in their early days, and to believe that they were full of the greatest promise for the race.

I have no intention of criticising the generosity and the noble self-sacrifice that produced them, nor the aspirations of their inmates. There is no doubt that they furnish shining examples of emancipation from ignorance, and of useful lives. But a few years have thrown much light upon the careers and characters of a great proportion of the graduates, and their effect upon the communities of which they form a part, I mean, of course, with regard to the industrial and moral condition of those communities. Have these colleges, as a whole,[1] stimulated industry, thrift, the inclination to settle down to the necessary hard work of the world, or have they bred idleness, indisposition to work, a vaporous ambition in politics, and that sort of conceit of gentility of which the world has already enough? If any one is in doubt about this he can satisfy himself by a sojourn in different localities in the south. The condition of New Orleans and its negro universities is often cited. It is a favourable example, because the ambition of the negro has been aided there by influence outside of the schools. The federal government has imposed upon the intelligent and sensitive population negro officials in high posi-

---

[1] This sentence should have been further qualified by acknowledging the excellent work done by the colleges at Atlanta and Nashville, which, under exceptionally good management, have sent out much-needed teachers. I believe that their success, however, is largely owing to their practical features. — *C. D. W.*

[213]

tions, because they were negroes and not because they were specially fitted for those positions by character or ability. It is my belief that the condition of the race in New Orleans is lower than it was several years ago, and that the influence of the higher education has been in the wrong direction.

This is not saying that the higher education is responsible for the present condition of the negro. Other influences have retarded his elevation and the development of proper character, and most important means have been neglected. I only say that we have been disappointed in our extravagant expectations of what this education could do for a race undeveloped, and so wanting in certain elements of character, and that the millions of money devoted to it might have been much better applied.

We face a grave national situation. It cannot be successfully dealt with sentimentally. It should be faced with knowledge and candour. We must admit our mistakes, both social and political, and set about the solution of our problem with intelligent resolution and a large charity. It is not simply a southern question. It is a northern question as well. For the truth of this I have only to appeal to the consciousness of all northern communities in which there are negroes in any considerable numbers. Have the negroes improved, as a rule (always remembering the exceptions), in thrift, truthfulness, morality, in the elements of industrious citizenship, even in States and towns where there has been the least prejudice against their education? In a paper read at the last session of this Association, Professor W. F. Willcox of Cornell University showed by statistics that in proportion to population there were more negro criminals in the north than in the south. "The negro prisoners in the southern States to ten thousand negroes increased between 1880 and 1890 twenty-nine per cent, while the white prisoners, to ten thousand whites increased only eight per cent." "In the States where slavery was never established, the white prisoners increased seven per cent faster than the white population, while the negro prisoners no less than thirty-nine per cent faster than the negro population. Thus the increase of negro criminality, so far as it is reflected in the number of prisoners, exceeded the increase of white criminality more in the north than it did in the south."

This statement was surprising. It cannot be accounted for by colour prejudice at the north; it is related to the known shiftlessness and irresponsibility of a great portion of the negro population. If it could be believed that this shiftlessness is due to the late state of slavery, the explanation would not do away with the existing conditions. Schools at the north have for a long time been open to the negro; though colour prejudice exists, he has not been on the whole in an unfriendly atmosphere, and willing hands have been stretched out to help him in his ambition to rise. It is no doubt true, as has been often said lately, that the negro at the north has been crowded out of many

occupations by more vigorous races, newly
come to this country, crowded out not only
of factory industries and agricultural, but of
the positions of servants, waiters, barbers,
and other minor ways of earning a living.
The general verdict is that this loss of position is due to lack of stamina and trust-
worthiness. Wherever a negro has shown
himself able, honest, attentive to the moral
and economic duties of a citizen, either successful in accumulating property or filling
honourably his station in life, he has gained
respect and consideration in the community
in which he is known; and this is as true at
the south as at the north, notwithstanding
the race antagonism is more accentuated by
reason of the preponderance of negro population there and the more recent presence
of slavery. Upon this ugly race antagonism
it is not necessary to enlarge here in discussing the problem of education, and I will
leave it with the single observation that I
have heard intelligent negroes, who were
honestly at work, accumulating property and
disposed to postpone active politics to a

more convenient season, say that they had nothing to fear from the intelligent white population, but only from the envy of the ignorant.

The whole situation is much aggravated by the fact that there is a considerable infusion of white blood in the negro race in the United States, leading to complications and social aspirations that are infinitely pathetic. Time only and no present contrivance of ours can ameliorate this condition.

I have made this outline of our negro problem in no spirit of pessimism or of prejudice, but in the belief that the only way to remedy an evil or a difficulty is candidly and fundamentally to understand it. Two things are evident: First, the negro population is certain to increase in the United States, in a ratio at least equal to that of the whites. Second, the south needs its labour. Its deportation is an idle dream. The only visible solution is for the negro to become an integral and an intelligent part of the industrial community. The way may be long, but he must work his way up. Sympathetic aid may do much, but the salvation of the negro is in his own hands, in the development of individual character and a race soul. This is fully understood by his wisest leaders. His worst enemy is the demagogue who flatters him with the delusion that all he needs for his elevation is freedom and certain privileges that were denied him in slavery.

In all the northern cities heroic efforts are made to assimilate the foreign population by education and instruction in Americanism. In the south, in the city and on plantation, the same effort is necessary for the negro, but it must be more radical and fundamental. The common school must be as fully sustained and as far reaching as it is in the north, reaching the lowest in the city slums and the most ignorant in the agricultural districts, but to its strictly elemental teaching must be added moral instructions, and training in industries and in habits of industry. Only by such rudimentary and industrial training can the mass of the negro race in the United States be expected to improve in character and position. A top-dressing of culture on a field with no depth of soil may for a moment stimulate the promise of vegetation, but no fruit will be produced. It is a gigantic task, and generations may elapse before it can in any degree be relaxed.

Why attempt it? Why not let things drift as they are? Why attempt to civilise the race within our doors, while there are so many distant and alien races to whom we ought to turn our civilising attention? The answer is simple and does not need elaboration. A growing ignorant mass in our body politic, inevitably cherishing bitterness of feeling, is an increasing peril to the public.

In order to remove this peril, by transforming the negro into an industrial, law-abiding citizen, identified with the prosperity of his country, the cordial assistance of the southern white population is absolutely essential. It can only be accomplished by regarding him as a man, with the natural right to the development of his capacity and

to contentment in a secure social state. The
effort for his elevation must be fundamental.
The opportunity of the common school must
be universal, and attendance in it compul-
sory. Beyond this, training in the decencies
of life, in conduct, and in all the industries,
must be offered in such industrial institutions as that of Tuskegee. For the exceptional cases a higher education can be easily
provided for those who show themselves
worthy of it, but not offered as an indis-
criminate panacea.

The question at once arises as to the kind
of teachers for these schools of various grades.
It is one of the most difficult in the whole
problem. As a rule, there is little gain,
either in instruction or in elevation of character, if the teacher is not the superior of the
taught. The learners must respect the
attainments and the authority of the teacher.
It is a too frequent fault of our common-
school system that, owing to inadequate pay
and ignorant selections, the teachers are not
competent to their responsible task. The
highest skill and attainment are needed to

evoke the powers of the common mind, even in a community called enlightened. Much more are they needed when the community is only slightly developed mentally and morally. The process of educating teachers of this race, fit to promote its elevation, must be a slow one. Teachers of various industries, such as agriculture and the mechanic arts, will be more readily trained than teachers of the rudiments of learning in the common schools. It is a very grave question whether, with some exceptions, the school and moral training of the race should not be for a considerable time to come in the control of the white race. But it must be kept in mind that instructors cheap in character, attainments, and breeding, will do more harm than good. If we give ourselves to this work, we must give of our best.

Without the cordial concurrence in this effort of all parties, black and white, local and national, it will not be fruitful in fundamental and permanent good. Each race must accept the present situation and build on it. To this end it is indispensable that one

great evil, which was inherent in the reconstruction measures and is still persisted in,
shall be eliminated. The party allegiance of
the negro was bid for by the temptation of
office and position for which he was in no
sense fit. No permanent, righteous adjustment of relations can come till this policy is
wholly abandoned. Politicians must cease
to make the negro a pawn in the game of
politics.

Let us admit that we have made a mistake.
We seem to have expected that we could
accomplish suddenly and by artificial contrivances a development which historically has
always taken a long time. Without abate-
ment of effort or loss of patience, let us put
ourselves in the common-sense, the scientific,
the historic line. It is a gigantic task, only
to be accomplished by long labour in accord
with the Divine purpose.

> " Thou wilt not leave us in the dust ;
> Thou madest man, he knows not why, —
> He thinks he was not made to die ;
> And thou hast made him ; thou art just.

" Oh, yet we trust that somehow good
Will be the final goal of ill,
To pangs of nature, sins of will,
Defects of doubt, and taints of blood.

" That nothing walks with aimless feet,
That not one life shall be destroyed,
Or cast as rubbish to the void,
When God hath made the pile complete."

The Indeterminate Sentence

WHAT SHALL BE DONE WITH THE CRIMINAL CLASS?

THE problem of dealing with the criminal class seems insolvable, and it undoubtedly is with present methods. It has never been attempted on a fully scientific basis, with due regard to the protection of society and to the interests of the criminal.

It is purely an economic and educational problem, and must rest upon the same principles that govern in any successful industry, or in education, and that we recognise in the conduct of life. That little progress has been made is due to public indifference to a vital question and to the action of sentimentalists, who, in their philanthropic zeal, fancy that a radical reform can come without radical discipline. We are largely wasting our energies in petty contrivances instead of striking at the root of the evil.

What do we mean by the "criminal class"? It is necessary to define this with some precision, in order to discuss intelligently the means of destroying this class. A criminal is one who violates a statute law, or, as we say, commits a crime. The human law takes cognisance of crime and not of sin. But all men who commit crime are not necessarily in the criminal class. Speaking technically, we put in that class those whose sole occupation is crime, who live by it as a profession, and who have no other permanent industry. They prey upon society. They are by their acts at war upon it, and are outlaws.

The State is to a certain extent responsible for this class, for it has trained most of them, from youth up, through successive detentions in lock-ups, city prisons, county jails, and in State prisons, and penitentiaries on relatively short sentences, under influences which tend to educate them as criminals and confirm them in a bad life. That is to say, if a man once violates the law and is caught, he is put into a machine from which it is very difficult for him to escape without further deterioration. It is not simply that the State puts a brand on him in the eyes of the community, but it takes away his self-respect without giving him an opportunity to recover it. Once recognised as in the criminal class, he has no further concern about the State than that of evading its penalties so far as is consistent with pursuing his occupation of crime.

To avoid misunderstanding as to the subject of this paper, it is necessary to say that it is not dealing with the question of prison reform in its whole extent. It attempts to consider only a pretty well-defined class. But in doing this it does not say that other aspects of our public peril from crime are not as important as this. We cannot relax our efforts in regard to the relations of poverty, drink, and unsanitary conditions, as leading to crime. We have still to take care of the exposed children, of those with parentage and surroundings inclining to crime, of the degenerate and the unfortunate. We have to keep up the warfare all along the line against the demoralisation of society. But we have here to deal with a specific manifestation; we have to capture a stronghold, the possession of which will put us in much better position to treat in detail the general evil.

Why should we tolerate any longer a professional criminal class? It is not large. It is contemptibly small compared with our seventy millions of people. If I am not mistaken, a late estimate gave us less than fifty thousand persons in our State prisons and penitentiaries. If we add to them those at large who have served one or two terms, and are generally known to the police, we shall not have probably more than eighty thousand of the criminal class. But call it a hundred thousand. It is a body that seventy millions of people ought to take care of with little difficulty. And we certainly ought to stop its increase. But we do not. The class grows every day. Those who watch the criminal reports are alarmed by the fact that an increasing number of those arrested for felonies are discharged convicts. This is an unmistakable evidence of the growth of the outlaw classes.

But this is not all. Our taxes are greatly increased on account of this class. We require more police to watch those who are at large and preying on society. We expend more yearly for apprehending and trying those caught, for the machinery of criminal justice, and for the recurring farce of imprisoning on short sentences and discharging those felons to go on with their work of swindling and robbing. It would be good economy for the public, considered as a taxpayer, to pay for the perpetual keep of these felons in secure confinement.

And still this is not the worst. We are all living in abject terror of these licensed robbers. We fear robbery night and day; we live behind bolts and bars (which should be reserved for the criminal) and we are in hourly peril of life and property in our homes and on the highways. But the evil does not stop here. By our conduct we are encouraging the growth of the criminal class, and we are inviting disregard of law, and diffusing a spirit of demoralisation through-out the country.

I have spoken of the criminal class as very limited; that is, the class that lives by the industry of crime alone. But it is not iso-lated, and it has widespread relations. There is a large portion of our population not tech-nically criminals, which is interested in main-taining this criminal class. Every felon is a part of a vast network of criminality. He has his dependents, his allies, his society of vice, all the various machinery of temptation and indulgence.

It happens, therefore, that there is great sympathy with the career of the lawbreakers, many people are hanging on them for sup-port, and among them the so-called criminal lawyers. Any legislation likely to interfere seriously with the occupation of the criminal class or with its increase is certain to meet with the opposition of a large body of voters. With this active opposition of those inter-ested, and the astonishing indifference of the general public, it is easy to see why so little is done to relieve us of this intolerable burden. The fact is, we go on increasing our expenses for police, for criminal procedure, for jails and prisons, and we go on increasing the criminal class and those affiliated with it.

And what do we gain by our present method? We do not gain the protection of society, and we do not gain the reformation of the criminal. These two statements do not admit of contradiction. Even those who cling to the antiquated notion that the business of society is to punish the offender must confess that in this game society is getting the worst of it. Society suffers all the time, and the professional criminal goes on with his occupation, interrupted only by periods of seclusion, during which he is comfortably housed and fed. The punishment he most fears is being compelled to relinquish his criminal career. The object of punishment for violation of statute law is not vengeance, it is not to inflict injury for injury. Only a few persons now hold to that. They say now that if it does little good to the offender, it is deterrent as to others. Now, is our present system deterrent? The statute law, no doubt, prevents many persons from committing crime, but our method of administering it certainly does not lessen the criminal class, and it does not adequately protect society. Is it not time we tried, radically, a scientific, a disciplinary, a really humanitarian method?

The proposed method is the indeterminate sentence. This strikes directly at the criminal class. It puts that class beyond the power of continuing its depredations upon society. It is truly deterrent, because it is a notification to any one intending to enter upon that method of living that his career ends with his first felony. As to the general effects of the indeterminate sentence, I will repeat here what I recently wrote for the *Yale Law Journal*:

It is unnecessary to say in a law journal that the indeterminate sentence is a measure as yet untried. The phrase has passed into current speech, and a considerable portion of the public is under the impression that an experiment of the indeterminate sentence is actually being made. It is, however, still a theory, not adopted in any legislation or in practice anywhere in the world.

The misconception in regard to this has arisen from the fact that under certain regulations paroles are granted before the expiration of the statutory sentence.

An indeterminate sentence is a commitment to prison without any limit. It is exactly such a commitment as the court makes to an asylum of a man who is proved to be insane, and it is paralleled by the practice of sending a sick man to the hospital until he is cured.

The introduction of the indeterminate sentence into our criminal procedure would be a radical change in our criminal legislation and practice. The original conception was that the offender against the law should be punished, and that the punishment should be made to fit the crime, an *opéra bouffe* conception which has been abandoned in reasoning though not in practice. Under this conception the criminal code was arbitrarily constructed, so much punishment being set down opposite each criminal offence, without the least regard to the actual guilt of the man as an individual sinner.

Within the present century considerable advance has been made in regard to prison reform, especially with reference to the sanitary condition of places of confinement. And besides this, efforts of various kinds have been made with regard to the treatment of convicts, which show that the idea was gaining ground that criminals should be treated as individuals. The application of the English ticket-of-leave system was one of these efforts; it was based upon the notion that, if any criminal showed sufficient evidence of a wish to lead a different life, he should be conditionally released before the expiration of his sentence. The parole system in the United States was an attempt to carry out the same experiment, and with it went along the practice which enabled the prisoner to shorten the time of his confinement by good behaviour. In some of the States reformatories have been established to which convicts have been sent under a sort of sliding sentence; that is, with the privilege given to the authorities of the reformatory to retain the offender to the full statutory term for which he might have been sentenced to State prison, unless he had evidently reformed before the expiration of that period. That is to say, if a penal offence entitled the judge to sentence the prisoner for any period from two to fifteen years, he could be kept in the reformatory at the discretion of the authorities for the full statutory term. It is from this law that the public notion of an indeterminate sentence is derived.

It is, in fact, determinate, because the statute prescribes its limit.

The introduction of the ticket-of-leave, and the parole systems, and the earning of time by good behaviour were philanthropic suggestions and promising experiments which have not been justified by the results. It is not necessary at this time to argue that no human discretion is adequate to mete out just punishment for crimes; and it has come to be admitted generally, by men enlightened on this subject, that the real basis for dealing with the criminal rests, firstly, upon the right of society to secure itself against the attacks of the vicious, and secondly, upon the duty imposed upon society, to reform the criminal if that is possible. It is patent to the most superficial observation that our present method does not protect society, and does not lessen the number of the criminal class, either by deterrent methods or by reformatory processes, except in a very limited way.

Our present method is neither economic nor scientific nor philanthropic. If we consider the well-defined criminal class alone, it can be said that our taxes and expenses for police and the whole criminal court machinery, for dealing with those who are apprehended, and watching those who are preying upon society, yearly increase, while all private citizens in their own houses or in the streets live in constant terror of the depredations of this class. Considered from the scientific point of view, our method is absolutely crude, and but little advance upon mediæval conditions; and while it has its sentimental aspects, it is not real philanthropy, because comparatively few of the criminal class are permanently rescued.

The indeterminate sentence has two distinct objects: one is the absolute protection of society from the outlaws whose only business in life is to prey upon society; and the second is the placing of these offenders in a position where they can be kept long enough for scientific treatment as decadent human beings, in the belief that their lives can be changed in their purpose. No specific time can be predicted in which a man by discipline can be expected to lay aside his bad habits and put on good habits, because no two human beings are alike, and it is therefore necessary that an indefinite time in each case should be allowed for the experiment of reformation.

We have now gone far enough to see that the ticket-of-leave system, the parole system as we administer it in the State prisons (I except now some of the reformatories), and the good conduct method are substantially failures, and must continue to be so until they rest upon the absolute indeterminate sentence. They are worse than failures now, because the public mind is lulled into a false security by them, and efforts at genuine prison reform are defeated.

It is very significant that the criminal class adapted itself readily to the parole system with its sliding scale. It was natural that this should be so, for it fits in perfectly well with their scheme of life. This is to them a sort of business career, interrupted now and then only by occasional limited periods of seclusion. Any device that shall shorten those periods is welcome to them. As a matter of fact, we see in the State prisons that the men most likely to shorten their time by good behaviour, and to get released on parole before the expiration of their sentence, are the men who make crime their career. They accept this discipline as a part of their lot in life, and it does not interfere with their business any more than the occasional bankruptcy of a merchant interferes with his pursuits.

It follows, therefore, that society is not likely to get security for itself, and the criminal class is not likely to be reduced essentially or reformed, without such a radical measure as the indeterminate sentence, which, accompanied, of course, by scientific treatment, would compel the convict to change his course of life, or to stay perpetually in confinement.　　[237]

Of course, the indeterminate sentence would radically change our criminal jurisprudence and our statutory provisions in regard to criminals. It goes without saying that it is opposed by the entire criminal class, and by that very considerable portion of the population which is dependent on or affiliated with the criminal class, which seeks to evade the law and escape its penalties. It is also opposed by a small portion of the legal profession which gets its living out of the criminal class, and it is sure to meet the objection of the sentimentalists who have peculiar notions about depriving a man of his liberty, and it also has to overcome the objections of many who are guided by precedents, and who think the indeterminate sentence would be an infringement of the judicial prerogative.

It is well to consider this latter a little further. Our criminal code, artificial and indiscriminating as it is, is the growth of ages and is the result of the notion that society ought to take vengeance upon the criminal, at least that it ought to punish him, and that the judge, the interpreter of the criminal law, was not only the proper person to determine the guilt of the accused, by the aid of the jury, but was the sole person to judge of the amount of punishment he should receive for his crime. Now two functions are involved here: one is the determination that the accused has broken the law, the other is gauging within the rules of the code the punishment that each individual should receive. It is a theological notion that the divine punishment for sin is somehow delegated to man for the punishment of crime, but it does not need any argument to show that no tribunal is able with justice to mete out punishment in any individual case, for probably the same degree of guilt does not attach to two men in the violation of the same statute, and while, in the rough view of the criminal law, even, one ought to have a severe penalty, the other should be treated with more leniency. All that the judge can do under the indiscriminating provisions of the statute is to make a fair guess at what the man should suffer.

Under the present enlightened opinion which sees that not punishment but the protection of society and the good of the criminal are the things to be aimed at, the judge's office would naturally be reduced to the task of determining the guilt of the man on trial, and then the care of him would be turned over to expert treatment, exactly as in a case when the judge determines the fact of a man's insanity.

If objection is made to the indeterminate sentence on the ground that it is an unusual or cruel punishment, it may be admitted that it is unusual, but that commitment to detention cannot be called cruel when the convict is given the key to the house in which he is confined. It is for him to choose whether he will become a decent man and go back into society, or whether he will remain a bad man and stay in confinement. For the criminal who is, as we might say, an accidental criminal, or for the criminal who is susceptible to good influences, the term of imprisonment under the indeterminate sentence would be shorter than it would be safe to make it for criminals under the statute. The incorrigible offender, however, would be cut off at once and forever from his occupation, which is, as we said, varied by periodic residence in the comfortable houses belonging to the State.

A necessary corollary of the indeterminate sentence is that every State prison and penitentiary should be a reformatory, in the modern meaning of that term. It would be against the interest of society, all its instincts of justice, and the height of cruelty to an individual criminal to put him in prison without limit unless all the opportunities were afforded him for changing his habits radically. It may be said in passing that the indeterminate sentence would be in itself to any man a great stimulus to reform, because his reformation would be the only means of his terminating that sentence. At the same time a man left to himself, even in the best ordered of our State prisons which is not a reformatory, would be scarcely likely to make much improvement.

I have not space in this article to consider the character of the reformatory; that subject is fortunately engaging the attention of scientific people as one of the most interesting of our modern problems. To take a decadent human being, a wreck physically and morally, and try to make a man of him, that is an attempt worthy of a people who claim to be civilised. An illustration of what can be done in this direction is furnished by the Elmira Reformatory, where the experiment is being made with most encouraging results, which, of course, would be still better if the indeterminate sentence were brought to its aid.

When the indeterminate sentence has been spoken of with a view to legislation, the question has been raised whether it should be applied to prisoners on the first, second, or third conviction of a penal offence. Legislation in regard to the parole system has also considered whether a man should be considered in the criminal class on his first conviction for a penal offence. Without entering upon this question at length, I will suggest that the convict should, for his own sake, have the indeterminate sentence applied to him upon conviction of his first penal offence. He is much more likely to reform then than he would be after he had had a term in the State prison and was again convicted, and the chance of his reformation would be lessened by each subsequent experience of this kind. The great object of the indeterminate sentence, so far as the security of society is concerned, is to diminish the number of the criminal class, and this will be done when it is seen that the first felony a man commits is likely to be his last, and that for a young criminal contemplating this career there is in this direction "no thoroughfare." By his very first violation of the statute he walks into confinement, to stay there until he has given up the purpose of such a career.

In the limits of this paper I have been obliged to confine myself to remarks upon the indeterminate sentence itself, without going into the question of the proper organisation of reformatory agencies to be applied to the convict, and without consideration of the means of testing the reformation of a man in any given case. I will only add that the methods at Elmira have passed far beyond the experimental stage in this matter.

The necessary effect of the adoption of the indeterminate sentence for felonies is that every State prison and penitentiary must be a reformatory. The convict goes into it for the term of a year at least (since the criminal law, according to ancient precedent, might require that, and because the discipline of the reformatory would require it as a practical rule), and he stays there until, in the judgment of competent authority, he is fit to be trusted at large.

If he is incapable of reform, he must stay there for his natural life. He is a free agent. He can decide to lead an honest life and have his liberty, or he can elect to work for the State all his life in criminal confinement.

When I say that every State prison is to be a reformatory, I except, of course, from its operation, those sentenced for life for murder, or other capital offences, and those who have proved themselves incorrigible by repeated violations of their parole.

It is necessary now to consider the treatment in the reformatory. Only a brief outline of it can be given here, with a general statement of the underlying principles. The practical application of these principles can be studied in the Elmira Reformatory of New York, the only prison for felons where the proposed system is carried out with the needed disciplinary severity. In studying Elmira, however, it must be borne in mind that the best effects cannot be obtained there, owing to the lack of the indeterminate sentence. In this institution the convict can only be detained for the maximum term provided in the statute for his offence. When that is reached, the prisoner is released, whether he is reformed or not.

The system of reform under the indeterminate sentence, which for convenience may be called the Elmira system, is scientific, and it must be administered entirely by trained men and by specialists; the same sort of training for the educational and industrial work as is required in a college or an industrial school, and the special fitness required for an alienist in an insane asylum. The discipline of the establishment must be equal to that of a military school.

We have so far advanced in civilisation that we no longer think of turning the insane, the sick, the feeble-minded, over to the care of men without training chosen by the chance of politics. They are put under specialists for treatment. It is as necessary that convicts should be under the care of specialists, for they are the most difficult and interesting subjects for scientific treatment. If not criminals by heredity, they are largely made so by environment; they are either physical degenerates or they are brutalised by vice. They have lost the power of distinguishing right from wrong; they commonly lack will-power, and so are incapable of changing their habits without external influence. In short, the ordinary criminal is unsound and diseased in mind and body.

To deal with this sort of human decadent is, therefore, the most interesting problem that can be offered to the psychologist, to the physiologist, to the educator, to the believer in the immortality of the soul. He is still a man, not altogether a mere animal, and there is always a possibility that he may be made a decent man, and a law-abiding, productive member of society.

Here, indeed, is a problem worthy of the application of all our knowledge of mind and of matter, of our highest scientific attainments. But it is the same problem that we have in all our education, be it the training of the mind, the development of the body, or the use of both to good ends. And it goes without saying that its successful solution, in a reformatory for criminals, depends upon the character of the man who administers the institution. There must be at the head of it a man of character, of intellectual force, of administrative ability, and all his subordinate officers must be fitted for their special task, exactly as they should be for a hospital, or a military establishment, for a college, or for a school of practical industries. And when such men are demanded, they will be forthcoming, just as they are in any department in life, when a business is to be developed, a great engineering project to be undertaken, or an army to be organised and disciplined.

The development of our railroad system produced a race of great railroad men. The protection of society by the removal and reform of the criminal class, when the public determines upon it, will call into the service a class of men fitted for the great work. We know this is so because already, since the discussion of this question has been current, and has passed into actual experiment, a race of workers and prison superintendents all over the country have come to the front who are entirely capable of administering the reform system under the indeterminate sentence. It is in this respect, and not in the erection of model prisons, that the great advance in penology has been made in the last twenty years. Men of scientific attainment are more and more giving their attention to this problem as the most important in our civilisation. And science is ready to take up this problem when the public is tired and ashamed of being any longer harried and bullied and terrorised over by the criminal class.

The note of this reform is *discipline*, and its success rests upon *the law of habit*. We are all creatures of habit, physical and mental. Habit is formed by repetition of any action. Many of our physical habits have become automatic. Without entering into a physiological argument, we know that repetition produces habit, and that, if this is long continued, the habit becomes inveterate. We know also that there is a habit, physical and moral, of doing right as well as doing wrong. The criminal has the habit of doing wrong. We propose to submit him to influences that will change that habit. We also know that this is not accomplished by suppressing that habit, but by putting a good one in its place.

It is true in this case that nature does not like a vacuum. The thoughts of men are not changed by leaving them to themselves, they are changed by substituting other thoughts.

The whole theory of the Elmira system is to keep men long enough under a strict discipline to change their habits. This discipline is administered in three ways. They are put to school; they are put at work; they are prescribed minute and severe rules of conduct, and in the latter training is included military drill.

The school and the workshop are both primarily for discipline and the formation of new habits. Only incidentally are the school and the workshop intended to fit a man for an occupation outside of the prison. The whole discipline is to put a man in possession of his faculties, to give him self-respect, to get him in the way of leading a normal and natural life. But it is true that what he acquires by the discipline of study and the discipline of work will be available in his earning an honest living. Keep a man long enough in this three-ply discipline, and he will form permanent habits of well-doing. If he cannot and will not form such habits, his place is in confinement, where he cannot prey upon society.

There is not space here to give the details of the practices at Elmira. They are easily attainable. But I will notice one or two objections that have been made. One is that in the congregate system men necessarily learn evil from each other. This is, of course, an evil. It is here, however, partially overcome by the fact that the inmates are kept so busy in the variety of discipline applied to them, that they have little or no time for anything else. They study hard, and are under constant supervision as to conduct. And then their prospect of parole depends entirely upon the daily record they make, and upon their radical change of intention. At night they are separated in their cells. During the day they are associated in class, in the workshop, and in drill, and this association is absolutely necessary to their training. In separation from their fellows, they could not be trained. Fear is expressed that men will deceive their keepers and the board which is to pass upon them, and obtain parole when they do not deserve it. As a matter of fact, men under this discipline cannot successfully play the hypocrite to the experts who watch them. It is only in the ordinary prison where the parole is in use with no adequate discipline, and without the indefinite sentence, that deception can be practised. But suppose a man does play the hypocrite so as to deceive the officers, who know him as well as any employer knows his workmen or any teacher knows his scholars, and deceives the independent board so as to get a parole. If he violates that parole, he can be remanded to the reformatory, and it will be exceedingly difficult for him to get another parole. And, if he should again violate his parole, he would be considered incorrigible and be placed in a life prison.

We have tried all other means of protecting society, of lessening the criminal class, of reforming the criminal. The proposed indeterminate sentence, with reformatory discipline, is the only one that promises to relieve society of the insolent domination and the terrorism of the criminal class; is the only one that can deter men from making a career of crime; is the only one that offers a fair prospect for the reformation of the criminal offender.

Why not try it? Why not put the whole system of criminal jurisprudence and procedure for the suppression of crime upon a sensible and scientific basis?

The Life-Saving and Life-Prolonging Art

IN the minds of the public there is a
mystery about the practice of medicine.
It deals more or less with the unknown,
with the occult, it appeals to the imagination. Doubtless confidence in its practitioners is still somewhat due to the belief
that they are familiar with the secret processes of nature, if they are not in actual
alliance with the supernatural. Investigation of the ground of the popular faith
in the doctor would lead us into metaphysics. And yet our physical condition
has much to do with this faith. It is apt
to be weak when one is in perfect health;
but when one is sick it grows strong. Saint
and sinner both warm up to the doctor
when the Judgment Day heaves in view.

In the popular apprehension the doctor is still the Medicine Man. We smile

when we hear about his antics in barbarous tribes; he dresses fantastically, he puts horns on his head, he draws circles on the ground, he dances about the patient, shaking his rattle and uttering incantations. There is nothing to laugh at. He is making an appeal to the imagination. And sometimes he cures, and sometimes he kills; in either case he gets his fee. What right have we to laugh? We live in an enlightened age, and yet a great proportion of the people, perhaps not a majority, still believe in incantations, have faith in ignorant practitioners who advertise a "natural gift," or a secret process or remedy, and prefer the charlatan who is exactly on the level of the Indian Medicine Man, to the regular practitioner, and to the scientific student of mind and body and of the properties of the *materia medica*. Why, even here in Connecticut, it is impossible to get a law to protect the community from the imposition of knavish or ignorant quacks, and to require of a man some evidence of capacity and training and skill, before he is let loose to experiment upon suffering humanity. Our teachers must pass an examination — though the examiner sometimes does not know as much as the candidate, — for misguiding the youthful mind; the lawyer cannot practise without study and a formal admission to the bar; and even the clergyman is not accepted in any responsible charge until he has given evidence of some moral and intellectual fitness. But the profession affecting directly the health and life of every human body, which needs to avail itself of the accumulated experience, knowledge, and science of all the ages, is open to every ignorant and stupid practitioner on the credulity of the public. Why cannot we get a law regulating the profession which is of most vital interest to all of us, excluding ignorance and quackery? Because the majority of our legislature, representing, I suppose, the majority of the public, believe in the " natural bone-setter," the herb doctor, the root doctor, the old woman who brews a decoction of swamp medicine, the " natural gift "

of some dabbler in diseases, the magnetic
healer, the faith cure, the mind cure, the
Christian Science cure, the efficacy of a
prescription rapped out on a table by some
hysterical medium, — in anything but sound
knowledge, education in scientific methods,
steadied by a sense of public responsibility.
Not long ago, on a cross-country road, I
came across a woman in a farmhouse,
where I am sure the barnyard drained into
the well, who was sick ; she had taken a
shop-full of patent medicines. I advised
her to send for a doctor. She had no
confidence in doctors, but said she reckoned she would get along now, for she
had sent for the seventh son of a seventh
son, and did n't I think he could certainly
cure her? I said that combination ought
to fetch any disease except agnosticism.
That woman probably influenced a vote
in the legislature. The legislature believes
in incantations; it ought to have in attendance an Indian Medicine Man.

We think the world is progressing in enlightenment; I suppose it is — inch by inch.

But it is not easy to name an age that has cherished more delusions than ours, or been more superstitious, or more credulous, more eager to run after quackery. Especially is this true in regard to remedies for diseases, and the faith in healers and quacks outside of the regular, educated professors of the medical art. Is this an exaggeration? Consider the quantity of proprietary medicines taken in this country, some of them harmless, some of them good in some cases, some of them injurious, but generally taken without advice and in absolute ignorance of the nature of the disease or the specific action of the remedy. The drug-shops are full of them, especially in country towns; and in the far west and on the Pacific coast I have been astonished at the quantity and variety displayed. They are found in almost every house; the country is literally dosed to death with these manufactured nostrums and panaceas — and that is the most popular medicine which can be used for the greatest number of internal and external diseases and injuries. Many newspapers are half sup-

17   [257]

ported by advertising them, and millions and millions of dollars are invested in this popular industry. Needless to say that the patented remedies most in request are those that profess a secret and unscientific origin. Those most "purely vegetable" seem most suitable to the wooden-heads who believe in them, but if one were sufficiently advertised as not containing a single trace of vegetable matter, avoiding thus all possible conflict of one organic life with another organic life, it would be just as popular. The favourites are those that have been secretly used by an East Indian fakir, or accidentally discovered as the natural remedy, dug out of the ground by an American Indian tribe, or steeped in a kettle by an ancient coloured person in a southern plantation, or washed ashore on the person of a sailor from the South Seas, or invented by a very aged man in New Jersey, who could not read, but had spent his life roaming in the woods, and whose capacity for discovering a "universal panacea," besides his ignorance and isolation, lay in the fact that his sands of life had nearly run. It is the sup-

posed secrecy or low origin of the remedy
that is its attraction. The basis of the vast
proprietary medicine business is popular
ignorance and credulity. And it needs to
be pretty broad to support a traffic of such
enormous proportions.

During this generation certain branches
of the life-saving and life-prolonging art
have made great advances out of empiri-
cism onto the solid ground of scientific
knowledge. Of course I refer to surgery,
and to the discovery of the causes and improvement in the treatment of contagious
and epidemic diseases. The general practice
has shared in this scientific advance, but it is
limited and always will be limited within experimental bounds, by the infinite variations
in individual constitutions, and the almost
incalculable element of the interference of
mental with physical conditions. When we
get an exact science of man, we may expect
an exact science of medicine. How far we
are from this, we see when we attempt to
make criminal anthropology the basis of
criminal legislation. Man is so complex

that if we were to eliminate one of his apparently worse qualities, we might develop others still worse, or throw the whole machine into inefficiency. By taking away what the phrenologists call combativeness, we could doubtless stop prize-fights, but we might have a springless society. The only safe way is that taught by horticulture, to feed a fruit-tree generously, so that it has vigour enough to throw off its degenerate tendencies and its enemies, or, as the doctors say in medical practice, bring up the general system. That is to say, there is more hope for humanity in stimulating the good, than in directly suppressing the evil. It is on something like this line that the greatest advance has been made in medical practice; I mean in the direction of prevention. This involves of course the exclusion of the evil, that is, of suppressing the causes that produce disease, as well as in cultivating the resistant power of the human system. In sanitation, diet, and exercise are the great fields of medical enterprise and advance. I need not say that the physician who, in the case of those under his charge, or who may possibly require his aid, contents himself with waiting for developed disease, is like the soldier in a besieged city, who opens the gates and then attempts to repel the invader who has effected a lodgment. I hope the time will come when the chief practice of the physician will be, first, in oversight of the sanitary condition of his neighbourhood, and, next, in preventive attendance on people who think they are well, and are all unconscious of the insidious approach of some concealed malady.

Another great change in modern practice is specialisation. Perhaps it has not yet reached the delicate particularity of the practice in ancient Egypt, where every minute part of the human economy had its exclusive doctor. This is inevitable in a scientific age, and the result has been on the whole an advance of knowledge, and improved treatment of specific ailments. The danger is apparent. It is that of the moral specialist, who has only one hobby and traces every human ill to strong liquor or tobacco, or the corset, or taxation of personal property, or denial of universal suffrage, or the eating of meat, or the want of the centralisation of nearly all initiative and interest and property in the state. The tendency of the accomplished specialist in medicine is to refer all physical trouble to the ill conduct of the organ he presides over. He can often trace every disease to want of width in the nostrils, to a defective eye, to a sensitive throat, to shut-up pores, to an irritated stomach, to an auricular defect. I suppose he is generally right, but I have a perhaps natural fear that if I happened to consult an amputationist about catarrh he would want to cut off my leg. I confess to an affection for the old-fashioned, all-round country doctor, who took a general view of his patient, knew his family, his constitution, all the gossip about his mental or business troubles, his affairs of the heart, disappointments in love, incompatibilities of temper, and treated the patient, as the phrase is, for all he was worth, and gave him visible medicine out of good old saddle-bags — how much faith we used to have in those saddle-bags — and not a prescription in a dead language to be put up by a dead-head clerk who occasionally mistakes arsenic for carbonate of soda. I do not mean, however, to say there is no sense in the retention of the hieroglyphics which the doctors use to communicate their ideas to a druggist, for I had a prescription made in Hartford put up in Naples, and that could not have happened if it had been written in English. And I am not sure but the mysterious symbols have some effect on the patient.

The mention of the intimate knowledge of family and constitutional conditions possessed by the old-fashioned country doctor, whose main strength lay in this and in his common-sense, reminds me of another great advance in the modern practice, in the attempt to understand nature better by the scientific study of psychology and the occult relations of mind and body. It is in the study of temper, temperament, hereditary predispositions, that we may expect the most brilliant results in preventive medicine.

As a layman, I cannot but notice another great advance in the medical profession. It is not alone in it. It is rather expected that the lawyers will divide the oyster between them and leave the shell to the contestants. I suppose that doctors, almost without exception, give more of their time and skill in the way of charity than almost any other profession. But somebody must pay, and fees have increased with the general cost of living and dying. If fees continue to increase as they have done in the past ten years in the great cities, like New York, nobody not a millionaire can afford to be sick. The fees will soon be a prohibitive tax. I cannot say that this will be altogether an evil, for the cost of calling medical aid may force people to take better care of themselves. Still, the excessive charges are rather hard on people in moderate circumstances who are compelled to seek surgical aid. And here we touch one of the regrettable symptoms of the times, which is not by any means most conspicuous in the medical profession. I mean the tendency to subordinate the old notion of professional duty to the greed for money. The lawyers are almost

universally accused of it; even the clergymen
are often suspected of being influenced by it.
The young man is apt to choose a profession
on calculation of its profit. It will be a bad
day for science and for the progress of the
usefulness of the medical profession, when
the love of money in its practice becomes
stronger than professional enthusiasm, than
the noble ambition of distinction for advan-
cing the science, and the devotion to human
welfare.

I do not prophesy it. Rather I expect interest in humanity, love of science for itself,
sympathy with suffering, self-sacrifice for
others, to increase in the world, and be
stronger in the end, than sordid love of gain
and the low ambition of rivalry in materialistic display. To this higher life the physician is called. I often wonder that there are
so many men, brilliant men, able men, with
so many talents for success in any calling,
willing to devote their lives to a profession
which demands so much self-sacrifice, so
much hardship, so much contact with suffering, subject to the call of all the world at

any hour of the day or night, involving so much personal risk, carrying so much heart-breaking responsibility, responded to by so much constant heroism, a heroism requiring the risk of life in a service the only glory of which is a good name and the approval of one's conscience.

To the members of such a profession, in spite of their human infirmities and limitations and unworthy hangers-on, I bow with admiration and the respect which we feel for that which is best in this world.

Literary Copyright

THIS is the first public meeting of
the National Institute of Arts and
Letters. The original members were
selected by an invitation from the American Social Science Association, which acted
under the power of its charter from the Congress of the United States. The members
thus selected, who joined the Social Science
Association, were given the alternative of
organising as an independent institute or as
a branch of the Social Science Association.

At the annual meeting of the Social
Science Association on September 4, 1899,
at Saratoga Springs, the members of the
Institute voted to organise independently.
They formally adopted the revised constitution, which had been agreed upon at the
first meeting, in New York in the preceding
January, and elected officers as prescribed by
the constitution.

The object is declared to be the advancement of art and literature, and the qualification shall be notable achievement in art or letters. The number of active members will probably be ultimately fixed at one hundred. The society may elect honorary and associate members without limit. By the terms of agreement between the American Social Science Association and the National Institute, the members of each are *ipso facto* associate members of the other.

It is believed that the advancement of art and literature in this country will be promoted by the organisation of the producers of literature and art. This is in strict analogy with the action of other professions and of almost all the industries. No one doubts that literature and art are or should be leading interests in our civilisation, and their dignity will be enhanced in the public estimation by a visible organisation of their representatives, who are seriously determined upon raising the standards by which the work of writers and artists is judged. The association of persons having this common aim cannot but stimulate effort, soften unworthy rivalry into generous competition, and promote enthusiasm and good fellowship in their work. The mere coming together to compare views and discuss interests and tendencies and problems which concern both the workers and the great public, cannot fail to be of benefit to both.

In no other way so well as by association of this sort can be created the feeling of solidarity in our literature, and the recognition of its power. It is not expected to raise any standard of perfection, or in any way to hamper individual development, but a body of concentrated opinion may raise the standard by promoting healthful and helpful criticism, by discouraging mediocrity and meretricious smartness, by keeping alive the traditions of good literature, while it is hospitable to all discoverers of new worlds. A safe motto for any such society would be Tradition and Freedom — *Traditio et Libertas.*

It is generally conceded that what literature in America needs at this moment is

honest, competent, sound criticism. This
is not likely to be attained by sporadic efforts, especially in a democracy of letters
where the critics are not always superior
to the criticised, where the man in front
of the book is not always a better marks-
man than the man behind the book. It
may not be attained even by an organisation of men united upon certain standards
of excellence. I do not like to use the word
authority, but it is not unreasonable to suppose that the public will be influenced by
a body devoted to the advancement of art
and literature, whose sincerity and discern-
ment it has learned to respect, and admission
into whose ranks will, I hope, be considered
a distinction to be sought for by good work.
The fashion of the day is rarely the judgment of posterity. You will recall what
Byron wrote to Coleridge: "I trust you
do not permit yourself to be depressed by
the temporary partiality of what is called
'the public' for the favourites of the moment;
all experience is against the permanency of
such impressions. You must have lived to

see many of these pass away, and will survive many more."

The chief concern of the National Institute is with the production of works of art and of literature, and with their distribution. In the remarks following I shall confine myself to the production and distribution of literature. In the limits of this brief address I can only in outline speak of certain tendencies and practices which are affecting this production and this distribution. The interests involved are, first, those of the author; second, those of the publisher; third, those of the public. As to all good literature, the interests of these three are identical if the relations of the three are on the proper basis. For the author, a good book is of more pecuniary value than a poor one, setting aside the question of fame; to the publisher, the right of publishing a good book is solid capital, — an established house, in the long run, makes more money on "Standards" than on "Catch-pennies;" and to the public the possession of the best literature is the breath of life, as that of the bad and mediocre is moral and intellectual decadence. But in practice the interests of the three do not harmonise. The author, even supposing his efforts are stimulated by the highest aspiration for excellence and not by any commercial instinct, is compelled by his circumstances to get the best price for his production; the publisher wishes to get the utmost return for his capital and his energy; and the public wants the best going for the least money.

Consider first the author, and I mean the author, and not the mere craftsman who manufactures books for a recognised market. His sole capital is his talent. His brain may be likened to a mine, gold, silver, copper, iron, or tin, which looks like silver when new. Whatever it is, the vein of valuable ore is limited, in most cases it is slight. When it is worked out the man is at the end of his resources. Has he expended or produced capital? I say he has produced it, and contributed to the wealth of the world, and that he is as truly entitled to the usufruct of it as the miner who takes gold or silver out of the earth. For how long? I will speak of that later on. The copyright of a book is not analogous to the patent right of an invention, which may become of universal necessity to the world. Nor should the greater share of this usufruct be absorbed by the manufacturer and publisher of the book. The publisher has a clear right to guard himself against risks, as he has the right of refusal to assume them. But there is an injustice somewhere, when for many a book, valued and even profitable to somebody, the author does not receive the price of a labourer's day wages for the time spent on it — to say nothing of the long years of its gestation.

The relation between author and publisher ought to be neither complicated nor peculiar. The author may sell his product outright, or he may sell himself by an agreement similar to that which an employee in a manufacturing establishment makes with his master to give to the establishment all his inventions. Either of these methods is fair and business-like, though it may not be wise. A method that prevailed in the early years of this century was both fair and wise. The author agreed that the publisher should have the exclusive right to publish his book for a certain term, or to make and sell a certain number of copies. When those conditions were fulfilled, the control of the property reverted to the author. The continuance of these relations between the two depended, as it should depend, upon mutual advantage and mutual good-will.

By the present common method the author makes over the use of his property to the will of the publisher. It is true that he parts with the use only of the property and not with the property itself, and the publisher in law acquires no other title, nor does he acquire any sort of interest in the future products of the author's brain. But the author loses all control of his property, and its profit to him may depend upon his continuing to make over his books to the same publisher. In this continuance he is liable to the temptation to work for a market, instead of following the free impulses of his own genius. As

to any special book the publisher is the sole
judge whether to push it or to let it sink
into the stagnation of unadvertised goods.

The situation is full of complications.
Theoretically it is the interest of both parties
to sell as many books as possible. But the
author has an interest in one book, the publisher in a hundred. And it is natural and
reasonable that the man who risks his money
should be the judge of the policy best for his
whole establishment. I cannot but think
that this situation would be on a juster
footing all round if the author returned to
the old practice of limiting the use of his
property by the publisher. I say this in full
recognition of the fact that the publishers
might be unwilling to make temporary investments, or to take risks. What then?
Fewer books might be published. Less
vanity might be gratified. Less money
might be risked in experiments upon the
public, and more might be made by distrib-
uting good literature. Would the public
be injured? It is an idea already discredited
that the world owes a living to everybody

who thinks he can write, and it is a superstition already fading that capital which
exploits literature as a trade acquires any
special privileges.

The present international copyright, which
primarily concerns itself with the manufacture of books, rests upon an unintelligible
protective tariff basis. It should rest primarily upon an acknowledgment of the
author's right of property in his own work,
the same universal right that he has in any
other personal property. The author's international copyright should be no more
hampered by restrictions and encumbrances
than his national copyright. Whatever regulations the government may make for the
protection of manufactures, or trade industries, or for purposes of revenue on importa-
tions, they should not be confounded with
the author's right of property. They have
no business in an international copyright act,
agreement, or treaty. The United States
copyright for native authors contains no
manufacturing restrictions. All we ask is
that foreign authors shall enjoy the same

privileges we have under our law, and that foreign nations shall give our authors the privileges of their local copyright laws. I do not know any American author of any standing who has ever asked or desired protection against foreign authors.

This subject is so important that I may be permitted to enlarge upon it, in order to make clear suggestions already made, and to array again arguments more or less familiar. I do this in the view of bringing before the institute work worthy of its best efforts, which if successful will entitle this body to the gratitude and respect of the country. I refer to the speedy revision of our confused and wholly inadequate American copyright laws, and later on to a readjustment of our international relations.

In the first place let me bring to your attention what is, to the vast body of authors, a subject of vital interest, which it is not too much to say has never received that treatment from authors themselves which its importance demands. I refer to the property of authors in their productions. In this brief space and time I cannot enter fully upon this great subject, but must be content to offer certain suggestions for your consideration.

The property of an author in the product of his mental labour ought to be as absolute and unlimited as his property in the product of his physical labour. It seems to me idle to say that the two kinds of labour products are so dissimilar that the ownership cannot be protected by like laws. In this age of enlightenment such a proposition is absurd. The history of copyright law seems to show that the treatment of property in brain product has been based on this erroneous idea. To steal the paper on which an author has put his brain work into visible, tangible form is in all lands a crime, larceny, but to steal the brain work is not a crime. The utmost extent to which our enlightened American legislators, at almost the end of the nineteenth century, have gone in protecting products of the brain has been to give the author power to sue in civil courts, at large

[278]

expense, the offender who has taken and sold his property.

And what gross absurdity is the copyright law which limits even this poor defence of authors' property to a brief term of years, after the expiration of which he or his children and heirs have no defence, no recognised property whatever in his products. And for some inexplicable reason this term of years in which he may be said to own his property is divided into two terms, so that at the end of the first he is compelled to re-assert his ownership by renewing his copyright, or he must lose all ownership at the end of the short term.

It is manifest to all honest minds that if an author is entitled to own his work for a term of years, it is equally the duty of his government to make that ownership perpetual. He can own and protect and leave to his children and his children's children by will, the manuscript paper on which he has written, and he should have equal right to leave to them that mental product which constitutes the true money value of his labour. It is unnecessary to say that the mental product is always as easy to be identified as the physical product. Its identification is absolutely certain to the intelligence of judges and juries. And it is apparent that the interests of assignees, who are commonly publishers, are equal with those of authors, in making absolute and perpetual this property in which both are dealers.

Another consideration follows here. Why should the ownership of a bushel of wheat, a piece of silk goods, a watch, or a handkerchief in the possession of an American carried or sent to England, or brought thence to this country, be absolute and unlimited, while the ownership of his own products as an author or as a purchaser from an author is made dependent on his nationality? Why should the property of the manufacturer of cloths, carpets, satins, and any and every description of goods, be able to send his products all over the world, subject only to the tariff laws of various countries, while the author (alone of all known producers) is forbidden to do so? The existing law of our country says to the foreign author, "You can have property in your book only if you manufacture it into saleable form in this country." What would be said of the wisdom or wild folly of a law which sought to protect other American industries by forbidding the importation of all foreign manufactures?

No question of tariff protection is here involved. What duty shall be imposed upon foreign products or foreign manufactures is a question of political economy. The wrong against which authors should protest is in annexing to their terms of ownership of their property a protective tariff provision. For, be it observed, this is a subject of abstract justice, moral right, and it matters nothing whether the author be American, English, German, French, Hindoo, or Chinese, — and it is very certain that when America shall enact a simple, just, copyright law, giving to every human being the same protection of law to his property in his mental products as in the work of his hands, every civilised nation on earth will follow the noble example.

As it now stands, authors who annually

produce the raw material for manufacturing purposes to an amount in value of millions, supporting vast populations of people, authors whose mental produce rivals and exceeds in commercial value many of the great staple products of our fields, are the only producers who have no distinct property in their products, who are not protected in holding on to the feeble tenure the law gives them, and whose quasi-property in their works, flimsy as it is, is limited to a few years, and cannot with certainty be handed down to their children.

It will be said, it is said, that it is impossible for the author to obtain an acknowledgment of absolute right of property in his brain work. In our civilisation we have not yet arrived at this state of justice. It may be so. Indeed some authors have declared that this justice would be against public policy. I trust they are sustained by the lofty thought that in this view they are rising above the petty realm of literature into the broad field of statesmanship.

But I think there will be a general agreement that in the needed revisal of our local copyright law we can attain some measure of justice. Some of the most obvious hardships can be removed. There is no reason why an author should pay for the privilege of a long life by the loss of his copyrights, and that his old age should be embittered by poverty because he cannot have the results of the labour of his vigorous years. There is no reason why if he dies young he should leave those dependent on him without support, for the public has really no more right to appropriate his book than it would have to take his house from his widow and children. His income at best is small after he has divided with the publishers.

No, there can certainly be no valid argument against extending the copyright of the author to his own lifetime, with the addition of forty or fifty years for the benefit of his heirs.

I will not leave this portion of the topic without saying that a perfectly harmonious relation between authors and publishers is most earnestly to be desired, nor without the

frank acknowledgment that, in literary tradition and in the present experience, many of
the most noble friendships and the most
generous and helpful relations have sub-
sisted, as they ought always to subsist, between the producers and the distributors of
literature, especially when the publisher has
a love for literature, and the author is a
reasonable being and takes pains to inform
himself about the publishing business.

One aspect of the publishing business
which has become increasingly prominent
during the last fifteen years cannot be over-
looked, for it is certain to affect seriously
the production of literature as to quality,
and its distribution. Capital has discovered
that literature is a product out of which
money can be made, in the same way that
it can be made in cotton, wheat, or iron.
Never before in history has so much money
been invested in publishing, with the single
purpose of creating and supplying the market with manufactured goods. Never before
has there been such an appeal to the reading
public, or such a study of its tastes, or sup-

posed tastes, wants, likes and dislikes, coupled also with the same shrewd anxiety to ascertain a future demand that governs the purveyors of spring and fall styles in millinery and dressmaking. Not only the contents of the books and periodicals, but the covers, must be made to catch the fleeting fancy. Will the public next season wear its hose dotted or striped?

Another branch of this activity is the so-called syndicating of the author's products in the control of one salesman, in which good work and inferior work are coupled together at a common selling price and in common notoriety. This insures a wider distribution, but what is its effect upon the quality of literature? Is it your observation that the writer for a syndicate, on solicitation for a price or an order for a certain kind of work, produces as good quality as when he works independently, uninfluenced by the spirit of commercialism? The question is a serious one for the future of literature.

The consolidation of capital in great publishing establishments has its advantages

[285]

and its disadvantages. It increases vastly the yearly output of books. The presses must be kept running, printers, paper-makers, and machinists are interested in this. The maw of the press must be fed. The capital must earn its money. One advantage of this is that when new and usable material is not forthcoming, the " standards " and the best literature must be reproduced in countless editions, and the best literature is broadcast over the world at prices to suit all purses, even the leanest. The disadvantage is that products, in the eagerness of competition for a market, are accepted which are of a character to harm and not help the development of the contemporary mind in moral and intellectual strength. The public expresses its fear of this in the phrase it has invented — " the spawn of the press." The author who writes simply to supply this press, and in constant view of a market, is certain to deteriorate in his quality, nay more, as a beginner he is satisfied if he can produce something that will sell without regard to its quality.

Is it extravagant to speak of a tendency to make the author merely an adjunct of the publishing house? Take as an illustration the publications in books and magazines relating to the late Spanish-American war. How many of them were ordered to meet a supposed market, and how many of them were the spontaneous and natural productions of writers who had something to say? I am not quarrelling, you see, with the newspapers who do this sort of thing; I am speaking of the tendency of what we have been accustomed to call literature to take on the transient and hasty character of the newspaper.

In another respect, in method if not in quality, this literature approaches the newspaper. It is the habit of some publishing houses, not of all, let me distinctly say, to seek always notoriety, not to nurse and keep before the public mind the best that has been evolved from time to time, but to offer always something new. The year's flooring is threshed off and the floor swept to make room for a fresh batch. Effort eventually

ceases for the old and approved, and is concentrated on experiments. This is like the
conduct of a newspaper. It is assumed that
the public must be startled all the time.

I speak of this freely because I think it as
bad policy for the publisher as it is harmful
to the public of readers. The same effort
used to introduce a novelty will be much
better remunerated by pushing the sale of an
acknowledged good piece of literature. Literature depends, like every other product
bought by the people, upon advertising, and
it needs much effort usually to arrest the
attention of our hurrying public upon what
it would most enjoy if it were brought to
its knowledge.

It would not be easy to fix the limit in
this vast country to the circulation of a good
book if it were properly kept before the
public. Day by day, year by year, new
readers are coming forward with curiosity
and intellectual wants. The generation that
now is should not be deprived of the best in
the last generation. Nay more, one publication, in any form, reaches only a compara-

tively small portion of the public that would be interested in it. A novel, for instance, may have a large circulation in a magazine; it may then appear in a book; it may reach other readers serially again in the columns of a newspaper; it may be offered again in all the by-ways by subscription, and yet not nearly exhaust its legitimate running power. This is not a supposition but a fact proved by trial. Nor is it to be wondered at, when we consider that we have an unequalled homogeneous population with a similar common-school education. In looking over publisher's lists I am constantly coming across good books out of print, which are practically unknown to this generation, and yet are more profitable, truer to life and character, more entertaining and amusing, than most of those fresh from the press month by month.

Of the effect upon the literary product of writing to order, in obedience to a merely commercial instinct, I need not enlarge to a company of authors, any more than to a company of artists I need to enlarge upon the effect of a like commercial instinct upon art.

I am aware that the evolution of literature or art in any period, in relation to the literature and art of the world, cannot be accurately judged by contemporaries and participants, nor can it be predicted. But I have great expectations of the product of both in this country, and I am sure that both will be affected by the conduct of persons now living. It is for this reason that I have spoken.

The Pursuit of Happiness

PERHAPS the most curious and interesting phrase ever put into a public document is "the pursuit of happiness." It is declared to be an inalienable right. It cannot be sold. It cannot be given away. It is doubtful if it could be left by will.

The right of every man to be six feet high, and of every woman to be five feet four, was regarded as self-evident, until women asserted their undoubted right to be six feet high also, when some confusion was introduced into the interpretation of this rhetorical fragment of the eighteenth century.

But the inalienable right to the pursuit of happiness has never been questioned since it was proclaimed as a new gospel for the New World. The American people accepted it with enthusiasm, as if it had been the discovery of a gold-prospector, and started out in the pursuit as if the devil were after them.

If the proclamation had been that happiness is a common right of the race, alienable or otherwise, that all men are or may be happy, history and tradition might have interfered to raise a doubt whether even the new form of government could so change the ethical condition. But the right to make a pursuit of happiness, given in a fundamental bill of rights, had quite a different aspect. Men had been engaged in many pursuits, most of them disastrous, some of them highly commendable. A sect in Galilee had set up the pursuit of righteousness as the only or the highest object of man's immortal powers. The rewards of it, however, were not always immediate. Here was a political sanction of a pursuit that everybody acknowledged to be of a good thing.

Given a heartaching longing in every human being for happiness, here was high warrant for going in pursuit of it. And the curious effect of this *mot d'ordre* was that the pursuit arrested the attention as the most essential, and the happiness was postponed, almost invariably, to some future season, when leisure or plethora, that is, relaxation or gorged desire, should induce that physical and moral glow which is commonly accepted as happiness. This glow of well-being is sometimes called contentment, but contentment was not in the programme. If it came at all, it was only to come after strenuous pursuit, that being the inalienable right.

People, to be sure, have different conceptions of happiness, but whatever they are, it is the custom, almost universal, to postpone the thing itself. This of course is specially true in our American system, where we have a chartered right to the thing itself. Other nations who have no such right may take it out in occasional driblets, odd moments that come, no doubt, to men and races who have no privilege of voting, or to such favoured places as New York city, whose government is always the same, however they vote.

We are all authorised to pursue happiness, and we do as a general thing make a pursuit of it. Instead of simply being happy in the condition where we are, getting the sweets of life in human intercourse, hour by hour, as the bees take honey from every flower that opens in the summer air, finding happiness in the well-filled and orderly mind, in the sane and enlightened spirit, in the self that has become what the self should be, we say that to-morrow, next year, in ten or twenty or thirty years, when we have arrived at certain coveted possessions or situation, we will be happy. Some philosophers dignify this postponement with the name of hope.

Sometimes wandering in a primeval forest, in all the witchery of the woods, besought by the kindliest solicitations of nature, wild flowers in the trail, the call of the squirrel, the flutter of birds, the great world-music of the wind in the pine-tops, the flecks of sunlight on the brown carpet and on the rough bark of immemorial trees, I find myself unconsciously postponing my enjoyment until I shall reach a hoped-for open place of full sun and boundless prospect.

The analogy cannot be pushed, for it is

the common experience that these open spots in life, where leisure and space and contentment await us, are usually grown up with thickets, fuller of obstacles, to say nothing of labours and duties and difficulties, than any part of the weary path we have trod.

Why add the pursuit of happiness to our other inalienable worries? Perhaps there is something wrong in ourselves when we hear the complaint so often that men are pursued by disaster instead of being pursued by happiness.

We all believe in happiness as something desirable and attainable, and I take it that this is the underlying desire when we speak of the pursuit of wealth, the pursuit of learning, the pursuit of power in office or in influence, that is, that we shall come into happiness when the objects last named are attained. No amount of failure seems to lessen this belief. It is matter of experience that wealth and learning and power are as likely to bring unhappiness as happiness, and yet this constant lesson of experience

[295]

makes not the least impression upon human conduct. I suppose that the reason of this unheeding of experience is that every person born into the world is the only one exactly of that kind that ever was or ever will be created, so that he thinks he may be exempt from the general rules. At any rate, he goes at the pursuit of happiness in exactly the old way, as if it were an original undertaking. Perhaps the most melancholy spectacle offered to us in our short sojourn in this pilgrimage, where the roads are so dusty and the caravansaries so ill provided, is the credulity of this pursuit. Mind, I am not objecting to the pursuit of wealth, or of learning, or of power, — they are all explainable, if not justifiable, — but to the blindness that does not perceive their futility as a means of attaining the end sought, which is happiness, an end that can only be compassed by the right adjustment of each soul to this and to any coming state of existence. For whether the great scholar who is stuffed with knowledge is happier than the great money-getter who is gorged with riches, or the wily politician who is a Warwick in his realm, depends entirely upon what sort of a man this pursuit has made him. There is a kind of fallacy current nowadays that a very rich man, no matter by what unscrupulous means he has gathered an undue proportion of the world into his possession, can be happy if he can turn round and make a generous and lavish distribution of it for worthy purposes. If he has preserved a remnant of conscience, this distribution may give him much satisfaction, and justly increase his good opinion of his own deserts; but the fallacy is in leaving out of account the sort of man he has become in this sort of pursuit. Has he escaped that hardening of the nature, that drying up of the sweet springs of sympathy, which usually attend a long-continued selfish undertaking? Has either he or the great politician or the great scholar cultivated the real sources of enjoyment?

The pursuit of happiness! It is not strange that men call it an illusion. But I am well satisfied that it is not the thing itself, but the pursuit, that is an illusion. Instead of thinking of the pursuit, why not fix our thoughts upon the moments, the hours, perhaps the days, of this divine peace, this merriment of body and mind, that can be repeated and perhaps indefinitely extended by the simplest of all means, namely, a disposition to make the best of whatever comes to us? Perhaps the Latin poet was right in saying that no man can count himself happy while in this life, that is, in a continuous state of happiness; but as there is for the soul no time save the conscious moment called "now," it is quite possible to make that "now" a happy state of existence. The point I make is that we should not habitually postpone that season of happiness to the future.

No one, I trust, wishes to cloud the dreams of youth, or to dispel by excess of light what are called the illusions of hope. But why should the boy be nurtured in the current notion that he is to be really happy only when he has finished school, when he has got a business or profession by which money can be made, when he has come to manhood? The girl also dreams that for her happiness lies ahead, in that springtime when she is crossing the line of womanhood, — all the poets make much of this, — when she is married and learns the supreme lesson how to rule by obeying. It is only when the girl and the boy look back upon the years of adolescence that they realise how happy they might have been then if they had only known they were happy, and did not need to go in pursuit of happiness.

The pitiful part of this inalienable right to the pursuit of happiness is, however, that most men interpret it to mean the pursuit of wealth, and strive for that always, postponing being happy until they get a fortune, and if they are lucky in that, find at the end that the happiness has somehow eluded them, that, in short, they have not cultivated that in themselves that alone can bring happiness. More than that, they have lost the power of the enjoyment of the essential pleasures of life. I think that the woman in the Scriptures who out of her poverty

[299]

put her mite into the contribution-box got more happiness out of that driblet of generosity and self-sacrifice than some men in our day have experienced in founding a university.

And how fares it with the intellectual man? To be a selfish miser of learning, for self-gratification only, is no nobler in reality than to be a miser of money. And even when the scholar is lavish of his knowledge in helping an ignorant world, he may find that if he has made his studies as a pursuit of happiness he has missed his object. Much knowledge increases the possibility of enjoyment, but also the possibility of sorrow. If intellectual pursuits contribute to an enlightened and altogether admirable character, then indeed has the student found the inner spring of happiness. Otherwise one cannot say that the wise man is happier than the ignorant man.

In fine, and in spite of the political injunction, we need to consider that happiness is an inner condition, not to be raced after. And what an advance in our situation it

would be if we could get it into our heads
here in this land of inalienable rights that
the world would turn round just the same
if we stood still and waited for the daily
coming of our Lord!

Truthfulness

TRUTHFULNESS is as essential in literature as it is in conduct, in fiction as it is in the report of an actual occurrence. Falsehood vitiates a poem, a painting, exactly as it does a life. Truthfulness is a quality like simplicity. Simplicity in literature is mainly a matter of clear vision and lucid expression, however complex the subject-matter may be; exactly as in life, simplicity does not so much depend upon external conditions as upon the spirit in which one lives. It may be more difficult to maintain simplicity of living with a great fortune than in poverty, but simplicity of spirit — that is, superiority of soul to circumstance — is possible in any condition. Unfortunately the common expression that a certain person has wealth is not so true as it would be to say that wealth has him. The life of one with great possessions and corresponding responsibilities may be full of complexity; the subject of literary art may be exceedingly complex; but we do not set complexity over against simplicity. For simplicity is a quality essential to true life as it is to literature of the first class; it is opposed to parade, to artificiality, to obscurity.

The quality of truthfulness is not so easily defined. It also is a matter of spirit and intuition. We have no difficulty in applying the rules of common morality to certain functions of writers for the public, for instance, the duties of the newspaper reporter, or the newspaper correspondent, or the narrator of any event in life the relation of which owes its value to its being absolutely true. The same may be said of hoaxes, literary or scientific, however clear they may be. The person indulging in them not only discredits his office in the eyes of the public, but he injures his own moral fibre, and he contracts such a habit of unveracity that he never can hope for genuine literary success. For there never was yet any genuine success in letters without integrity. The clever hoax is no better than the trick of imitation, that is, conscious imitation of another, which has unveracity to one's self at the bottom of it. Burlesque is not the highest order of intellectual performance, but it is legitimate, and if cleverly done it may be both useful and amusing, but it is not to be confounded with forgery, that is, with a composition which the author attempts to pass off as the production of somebody else. The forgery may be amazingly smart, and be even popular, and get the author, when he is discovered, notoriety, but it is pretty certain that with his ingrained lack of integrity he will never accomplish any original work of value, and he will be always personally suspected. There is nothing so dangerous to a young writer as to begin with hoaxing; or to begin with the invention, either as reporter or correspondent, of statements put forward as facts, which are untrue. This sort of facility and smartness may get a writer employment, unfortunately for him and the public, but there is no satisfaction in it to

one who desires an honourable career. It
is easy to recall the names of brilliant men
whose fine talents have been eaten away by
this habit of unveracity. This habit is the
greatest danger of the newspaper press of
the United States.

It is easy to define this sort of untruthful-
ness, and to study the moral deterioration it
works in personal character, and in the
quality of literary work. It was illustrated
in the forgeries of the marvellous boy Chat-
terton. The talent he expended in deception
might have made him an enviable reputation,
— the deception vitiated whatever good there
was in his work. Fraud in literature is no
better than fraud in archæology, — Chatter-
ton deserves no more credit than Shapiro
who forged the Moabite pottery with its
inscriptions. The reporter who invents an
incident, or heightens the horror of a calam-
ity by fiction is in the case of Shapiro. The
habit of this sort of invention is certain to
destroy the writer's quality, and if he attempts a legitimate work of the imagination,
he will carry the same unveracity into that.

The quality of truthfulness cannot be juggled with. Akin to this is the trick which has put under proper suspicion some very clever writers of our day, and cost them all public confidence in whatever they do, — the trick of posing for what they are not. We do not mean only that the reader does not believe their stories of personal adventure, and regards them personally as " frauds," but that this quality of deception vitiates all their work, as seen from a literary point of view. We mean that the writer who hoaxes the public, by inventions which he publishes as facts, or in regard to his own personality, not only will lose the confidence of the public but he will lose the power of doing genuine work, even in the field of fiction. Good work is always characterised by integrity.

These illustrations help us to understand what is meant by literary integrity. For the deception in the case of the correspondent who invents " news " is of the same quality as the lack of sincerity in a poem or in a prose fiction; there is a moral and probably a mental defect in both. The story of Robinson Crusoe is a very good illustration of veracity in fiction. It is effective because it has the simple air of truth; it is an illusion that satisfies; it is possible; it is good art: but it has no moral deception in it. In fact, looked at as literature, we can see that it is sincere and wholesome.

What is this quality of truthfulness which we all recognise when it exists in fiction? There is much fiction, and some of it, for various reasons, that we like and find interesting which is nevertheless insincere if not artificial. We see that the writer has not been honest with himself or with us in his views of human life. There may be just as much lying in novels as anywhere else. The novelist who offers us what he declares to be a figment of his own brain may be just as untrue as the reporter who sets forth a figment of his own brain which he declares to be a real occurrence. That is, just as much faithfulness to life is required of the novelist as of the reporter, and in a much higher degree. The novelist must not only tell the truth about life as he sees it, material and spiritual, but he must be faithful to his own conceptions. If fortunately he has genius enough to create a character that has reality to himself and to others, he must be faithful to that character. He must have conscience about it, and not misrepresent it, any more than he would misrepresent the sayings and doings of a person in real life. Of course if his own conception is not clear, he will be as unjust as in writing about a person in real life whose character he knew only by rumour. The novelist may be mistaken about his own creations and in his views of life, but if he have truthfulness in himself, sincerity will show in his work.

Truthfulness is a quality that needs to be as strongly insisted on in literature as simplicity. But when we carry the matter a step further, we see that there cannot be truthfulness about life without knowledge. The world is full of novels, and their number daily increases, written without any sense of responsibility, and with very little experience, which are full of false views of human nature

and of society. We can almost always tell
in a fiction when the writer passes the boun-
dary of his own experience and observation
— he becomes unreal, which is another name
for untruthful. And there is an absence of
sincerity in such work. There seems to be
a prevailing impression that any one can
write a story. But it scarcely need be said
that literature is an art, like painting and
music, and that one may have knowledge of
life and perfect sincerity, and yet be unable to
produce a good, truthful piece of literature,
or to compose a piece of music, or to paint a
picture.

Truthfulness is in no way opposed to invention or to the exercise of the imagination.
When we say that the writer needs experience, we do not mean to intimate that his
invention of character or plot should be literally limited to a person he has known, or to
an incident that has occurred, but that they
should be true to his experience. The writer
may create an ideally perfect character, or an
ideally bad character, and he may try him by
a set of circumstances and events never

before combined, and this creation may be so romantic as to go beyond the experience of any reader, that is to say, wholly imaginary (like a composed landscape which has no counterpart in any one view of a natural landscape), and yet it may be so consistent in itself, so true to an idea or an aspiration or a hope, that it will have the element of truthfulness and subserve a very high purpose. It may actually be truer to our sense of verity to life than an array of undeniable, naked facts set down without art and without imagination.

The difficulty of telling the truth in literature is about as great as it is in real life. We know how nearly impossible it is for one person to convey to another a correct impression of a third person. He may describe the features, the manner, mention certain traits and sayings, all literally true, but absolutely misleading as to the total impression. And this is the reason why extreme, unrelieved realism is apt to give a false impression of persons and scenes. One can hardly help having a whimsical notion occasionally, seeing the miscarriages even in our own attempts at truthfulness, that it absolutely exists only in the imagination.

In a piece of fiction, especially romantic fiction, an author is absolutely free to be truthful, and he will be if he has personal and literary integrity. He moves freely amid his own creations and conceptions, and is not subject to the peril of the writer who admittedly uses facts, but uses them so clumsily or with so little conscience, so out of their real relations, as to convey a false impression and an untrue view of life. This quality of truthfulness is equally evident in "The Three Guardsmen" and in "Midsummer Night's Dream." Dumas is as conscientious about his world of adventure as Shakespeare is in his semi-supernatural region. If Shakespeare did not respect the laws of his imaginary country, and the creatures of his fancy, if Dumas were not true to the characters he conceived, and the achievements possible to them, such works would fall into confusion. A recent story called "The Refugees" set out with a certain promise of veracity, although the reader understood of course that it was to be a purely romantic invention. But very soon the author recklessly violated his own conception, and when he got his "real" characters upon an iceberg, the fantastic position became ludicrous without being funny, and the performances of the same characters in the wilderness of the New World showed such lack of knowledge in the writer that the story became an insult to the intelligence of the reader. Whereas such a romance as that of "The MS. Found in a Copper Cylinder," although it is humanly impossible and visibly a figment of the imagination, is satisfactory to the reader because the author is true to his conception, and it is interesting as a curious allegorical and humorous illustration of the ruinous character in human affairs of extreme unselfishness. There is the same sort of truthfulness in Hawthorne's allegory of "The Celestial Railway," in Froude's "On a Siding at a Railway Station," and in Bunyan's "Pilgrim's Progress."

The habit of lying carried into fiction

vitiates the best work, and perhaps it is easier to avoid it in pure romance than in the so-called novels of "every-day life." And this is probably the reason why so many of the novels of "real life" are so much more offensively untruthful to us than the wildest romances. In the former the author could perhaps "prove" every incident he narrates, and produce living every character he has attempted to describe. But the effect is that of a lie, either because he is not a master of his art, or because he has no literary conscience. He is like an artist who is more anxious to produce a meretricious effect than he is to be true to himself or to nature. An author who creates a character assumes a great responsibility, and if he has not integrity or knowledge enough to respect his own creation, no one else will respect it, and, worse than this, he will tell a falsehood to hosts of undiscriminating readers.

Literature and the Stage

IS the divorce of Literature and the Stage complete, or is it still only partial? As the lawyers say, is it *a vinculo*, or only *a mensa et thoro?* And if this divorce is permanent, is it a good thing for literature or the stage? Is the present condition of the stage a degeneration, as some say, or is it a natural evolution of an art independent of literature?

How long is it since a play has been written and accepted and played which has in it any so-called literary quality or is an addition to literature? And what is dramatic art as at present understood and practised by the purveyors of plays for the public? If any one can answer these questions, he will contribute something to the discussion about the tendency of the modern stage.

Every one recognises in the "good old plays" which are occasionally "revived" both a quality and an intention different from anything in most contemporary productions. They are real dramas, the interest of which depends upon sentiment, upon an exhibition of human nature, upon the interaction of varied character, and upon plot, and we recognise in them a certain literary art. They can be read with pleasure. Scenery and mechanical contrivance may heighten the effects, but they are not absolute essentials.

In the contemporary play instead of character we have " characters," usually exaggerations of some trait, so pushed forward as to become caricatures. Consistency to human nature is not insisted on in plot, but there must be startling and unexpected incidents, mechanical devices, and a great deal of what is called "business," which clearly has as much relation to literature as have the steps of a *farceur* in a clog-dance. The composition of such plays demands literary ability in the least degree, but ingenuity in inventing situations and surprises; the text is nothing, the action is everything; but the text is considerably improved if it have brightness of repartee and a lively apprehension of contemporary events, including the slang of the hour. These plays appear to be made up by the writer, the manager, the carpenter, the costumer. If they are successful with the modern audiences, their success is probably due to other things than any literary quality they may have, or any truth to life or to human nature.

We see how this is in the great number of plays adapted from popular novels. In the " dramatisation " of these stories, pretty much everything is left out of the higher sort that the reader has valued in the story. The romance of " Monte Cristo " is an illustration of this. The play is vulgar melodrama, out of which has escaped altogether the refinement and the romantic idealism of the stirring romance of Dumas. Now and then, to be sure, we get a different result, as in " Olivia," where all the pathos and character of the " Vicar of Wakefield " are preserved, and the effect of the play depends upon passion and sentiment. But as a rule, we get only the more obvious saliencies, the bones of the novel, fitted in or clothed with stage "business."

Of course it is true that literary men, even dramatic authors, may write and always have written dramas not suited to actors, that could not well be put upon the stage. But it remains true that the greatest dramas, those that have endured from the Greek times down, have been (for the audiences of their times) both good-reading and good-acting plays.

I am not competent to criticise the stage or its tendency. But I am interested in noticing the increasing non-literary character of modern plays. It may be explained as a necessary and justifiable evolution of the stage. The managers may know what the audience wants, just as the editors of some of the most sensational newspapers say that they make a newspaper to suit the public. The newspaper need not be well written, but it must startle with incident and surprise, found or invented. An observer must notice that the usual theatre-audience in New York or Boston to-day laughs at and applauds costumes, situations, innuendoes, doubtful suggestions, that it would have blushed at a few years ago. Has the audience been creating a theatre to suit its taste, or have the managers been educating an audience? Has the divorce of literary art from the mimic art of the stage anything to do with this condition?

The stage can be amusing, but can it show life as it is without the aid of idealising literary art? And if the stage goes on in this materialistic way, how long will it be before it ceases to amuse intelligent, not to say intellectual people?

"H. H." in Southern California

I T seems somehow more nearly an irrep-
arable loss to us than to "H. H." that
she did not live to taste her very substantial fame in Southern California. We should
have had such delight in her unaffected
pleasure in it, and it would have been one
of those satisfactions somewhat adequate
to our sense of fitness that are so seldom
experienced. It was my good fortune to
see Mrs. Jackson frequently in the days in
New York when she was writing "Ramona,"
which was begun and perhaps finished in
the Berkeley House. The theme had complete possession of her, and chapter after
chapter flowed from her pen as easily as
one would write a letter to a friend; and
she had an ever fresh and vigorous delight
in it. I have often thought that no one

enjoyed the sensation of living more than
Mrs. Jackson, or was more alive to all the
influences of nature and the contact of
mind with mind, more responsive to all
that was exquisite and noble either in nature or in society, or more sensitive to the
disagreeable. This is merely saying that
she was a poet; but when she became interested in the Indians, and especially in
the harsh fate of the Mission Indians in
California, all her nature was fused for the
time in a lofty enthusiasm of pity and in-
dignation, and all her powers seemed to be
consecrated to one purpose. Enthusiasm
and sympathy will not make a novel, but
all the same they are necessary to the production of a work that has in it real vital
quality, and in this case all previous experience and artistic training became the unconscious servants of Mrs. Jackson's heart.
I know she had very little conceit about
her performance, but she had a simple
consciousness that she was doing her best
work, and that if the world should care
much for anything she had done, after she

was gone, it would be for "Ramona." She
had put herself into it.

And yet I am certain that she could
have had no idea what the novel would be
to the people of Southern California, or
how it would identify her name with all
that region, and make so many scenes in
it places of pilgrimage and romantic interest for her sake. I do not mean to say
that the people in California knew personally Ramona and Alessandro, or altogether
believe in them, but that in their idealisa-
tions they recognise a verity and the ultimate truth of human nature, while in the
scenery, in the fading sentiment of the old
Spanish life, and the romance and faith of
the Missions, the author has done for the
region very much what Scott did for the
Highlands. I hope she knows now, I pre-
sume she does, that more than one Indian
school in the Territories is called the Ramona School; that at least two villages in
California are contending for the priority
of using the name Ramona; that all the
travellers and tourists (at least in the time

they can spare from real-estate specula-
tions) go about under her guidance, are
pilgrims to the shrines she has described,
and eager searchers for the scenes she has
made famous in her novel; that more than
one city and more than one town claims
the honour of connection with the story;
that the tourist has pointed out to him in
more than one village the very house
where Ramona lived, where she was married — indeed, that a little crop of legends
has already grown up about the story itself.   I was myself shown the house in
Los Angeles where the story was written,
and so strong is the local impression that
I confess to looking at the rose-embow-
ered cottage with a good deal of interest,
though I had seen the romance growing
day by day in the Berkeley in New York.

The undoubted scene of the loves of
Ramona and Alessandro is the Comulos
rancho, on the railway from Newhall to
Santa Paula, the route that one takes now
(unless he wants to have a life-long remem-
brance of the ground swells of the Pacific in

an uneasy little steamer) to go from Los
Angeles to Santa Barbara. It is almost the
only one remaining of the old-fashioned
Spanish haciendas, where the old administration prevails. The new railway passes it
now, and the hospitable owners have been
obliged to yield to the public curiosity and
provide entertainment for a continual stream
of visitors. The place is so perfectly described in "Ramona" that I do not need
to draw it over again, and I violate no confidence and only certify to the extraordinary
powers of delineation of the novelist, when I
say that she only spent a few hours there, —
not a quarter of the time we spent in iden-
tifying her picture. We knew the situation before the train stopped by the crosses erected
on the conspicuous peaks of the serrated
ashy — or shall I say purple — hills that en-
fold the fertile valley. It is a great domain,
watered by a swift river, and sheltered by
wonderfully picturesque mountains. The
house is strictly in the old Spanish style,
of one story about a large court, with flowers
and a fountain, in which are the most noisy

if not musical frogs in the world, and all the interior rooms opening upon a gallery. The real front is towards the garden, and here at the end of the gallery is the elevated room where Father Salvierderra slept when he passed a night at the hacienda, — a pretty room which has a case of Spanish books, mostly religious and legal, and some quaint and cheap holy pictures. We had a letter to Signora Del Valle, the mistress, and were welcomed with a sort of formal extension of hospitality that put us back into the courtly manners of a hundred years ago. The Signora, who is in no sense the original of the mistress whom " H. H." describes, is a widow now for seven years, and is the vigilant administrator of all her large domain, of the stock, the grazing lands, the vineyard, the sheep ranch, and all the people. Rising very early in the morning, she visits every department, and no detail is too minute to escape her inspection, and no one in the great household but feels her authority.

It was a very lovely day on the 17th of March (indeed, I suppose it had been pre-

ceded by 364 days exactly like it) as we sat
upon the gallery looking on the garden, a
garden of oranges, roses, citrons, lemons,
peaches — what fruit and flower was not
growing there? — acres and acres of vineyard
beyond, with the tall cane and willows by the
stream, and the purple mountains against
the sapphire sky. Was there ever anything
more exquisite than the peach-blossoms
against that blue sky! Such a place of
peace. A soft south wind was blowing, and
all the air was drowsy with the hum of bees.
In the garden is a vine-covered arbour, with
seats and tables, and at the end of it is
the opening into a little chapel, a domestic
chapel, carpeted like a parlour, and bearing
all the emblems of a loving devotion. By
the garden gate hang three small bells,
from some old mission, all cracked, but serv-
ing (each has its office) to summon the workmen or to call to prayer.

Perfect system reigns in Signora Del
Valle's establishment, and even the least
child in it has its duty. At sundown a little
slip of a girl went out to the gate and struck

one of the bells. "What is that for?" I
asked as she returned. "It is the Angelus,"
she said simply. I do not know what would
happen to her if she should neglect to strike
it at the hour. At eight o'clock the largest
bell was struck, and the Signora and all her
household, including the house servants, went
out to the little chapel in the garden, which
was suddenly lighted with candles, gleaming
brilliantly through the orange groves. The
Signora read the service, the household re-
sponding — a twenty minutes' service, which
is as much a part of the administration of the
establishment as visiting the granaries and
presses, and the bringing home of the goats.
The Signora's apartments, which she permitted us to see, were quite in the nature
of an oratory, with shrines and sacred pictures and relics of the faith. By the shrine
at the head of her bed hung the rosary carried by Father Junipero, — a priceless possession. From her presses and armoires, the
Signora, seeing we had a taste for such
things, brought out the feminine treasures
of three generations, the silk and embroidered

dresses of last century, the ribosas, the jewelry, the brilliant stuffs of China and Mexico, each article with a memory and a flavour.

But I must not be betrayed into writing about Ramona's house. How charming indeed it was the next morning, — tho' the birds in the garden were astir a little too early, — with the thermometer set to the exact degree of warmth without languor, the sky blue, the wind soft, the air scented with orange and jessamine. The Signora had already visited all her premises before we were up. We had seen the evening before an enclosure near the house full of cashmere goats and kids, whose antics were sufficiently amusing — most of them had now gone afield; workmen were coming for their orders, ploughing was going on in the barley fields, traders were driving to the plantation store, the fierce eagle in a big cage by the olive press was raging at his detention. Within the house enclosure are an olive mill and press, a wine-press and a great storehouse of wine, containing now little but empty casks, — a dusky, interesting place, with pomegranates and dried bunches of grapes and oranges and pieces of jerked meat hanging from the rafters. Near by is a corn-house and a small distillery, and the corrals for sheep shearing are not far off. The ranches for cattle and sheep are on the other side of the mountain.

Peace be with Comulos. It must please the author of "Ramona" to know that it continues in the old ways; and I trust she is undisturbed by the knowledge that the rage for change will not long let it be what it now is.